THIS COLOURING BOOK BELONGS TO:

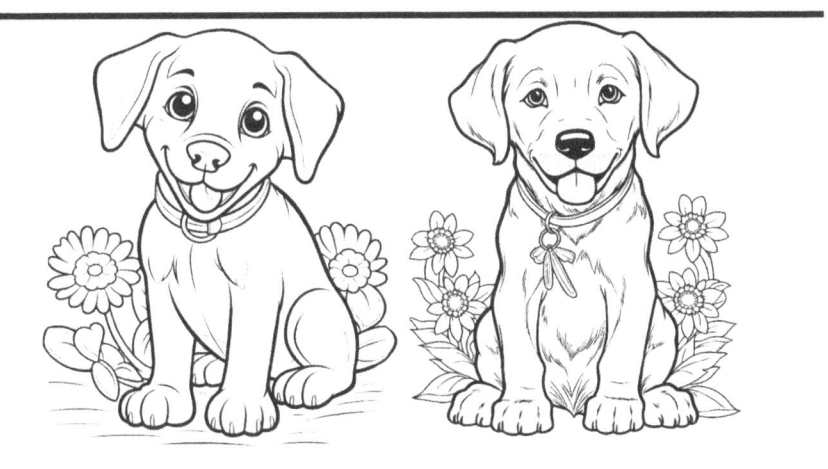

Introduction

Welcome to the Wonderful World of Coloring!

Dive into an adventure of colors, imagination, and creativity with this special coloring book made just for you! Inside these pages, you'll find a magical world waiting to be brought to life by your colorful imagination. From friendly animals to enchanting landscapes, there's no limit to what you can create.

Grab your favorite crayons, markers, or colored pencils, and get ready to embark on a journey where the only limit is your imagination! So, let your creativity soar, add splashes of color to each page, and watch as your masterpieces come to life before your eyes.

Let the coloring fun begin!

0.

I'm a playful cat who enjoys licking my paws and snoozing all day!

zZz

1.

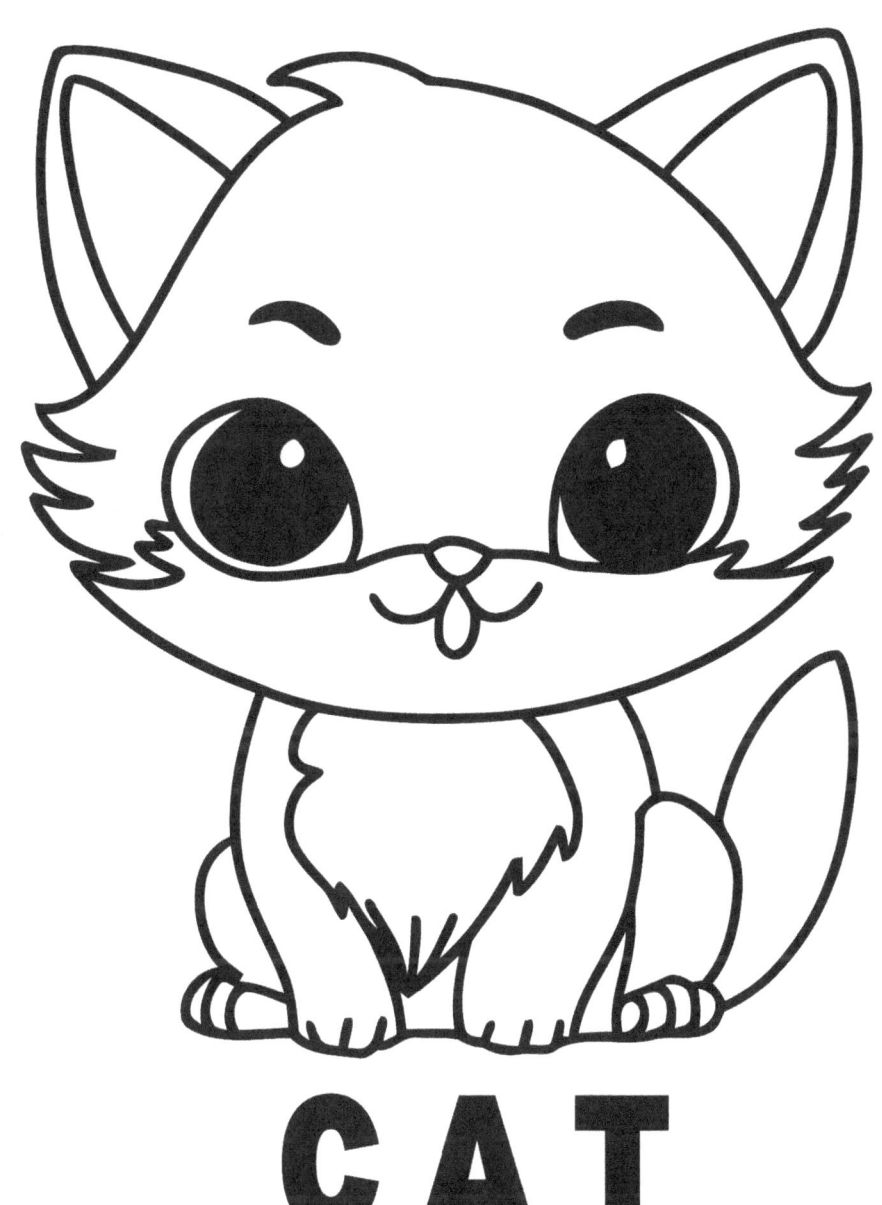

2. **CAT**

I'm a happy doggie who loves to woof at the cars as they zoom past!

3.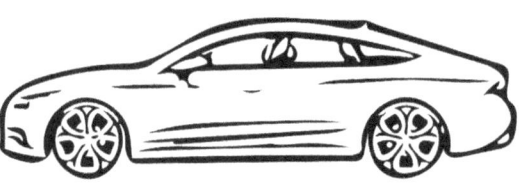

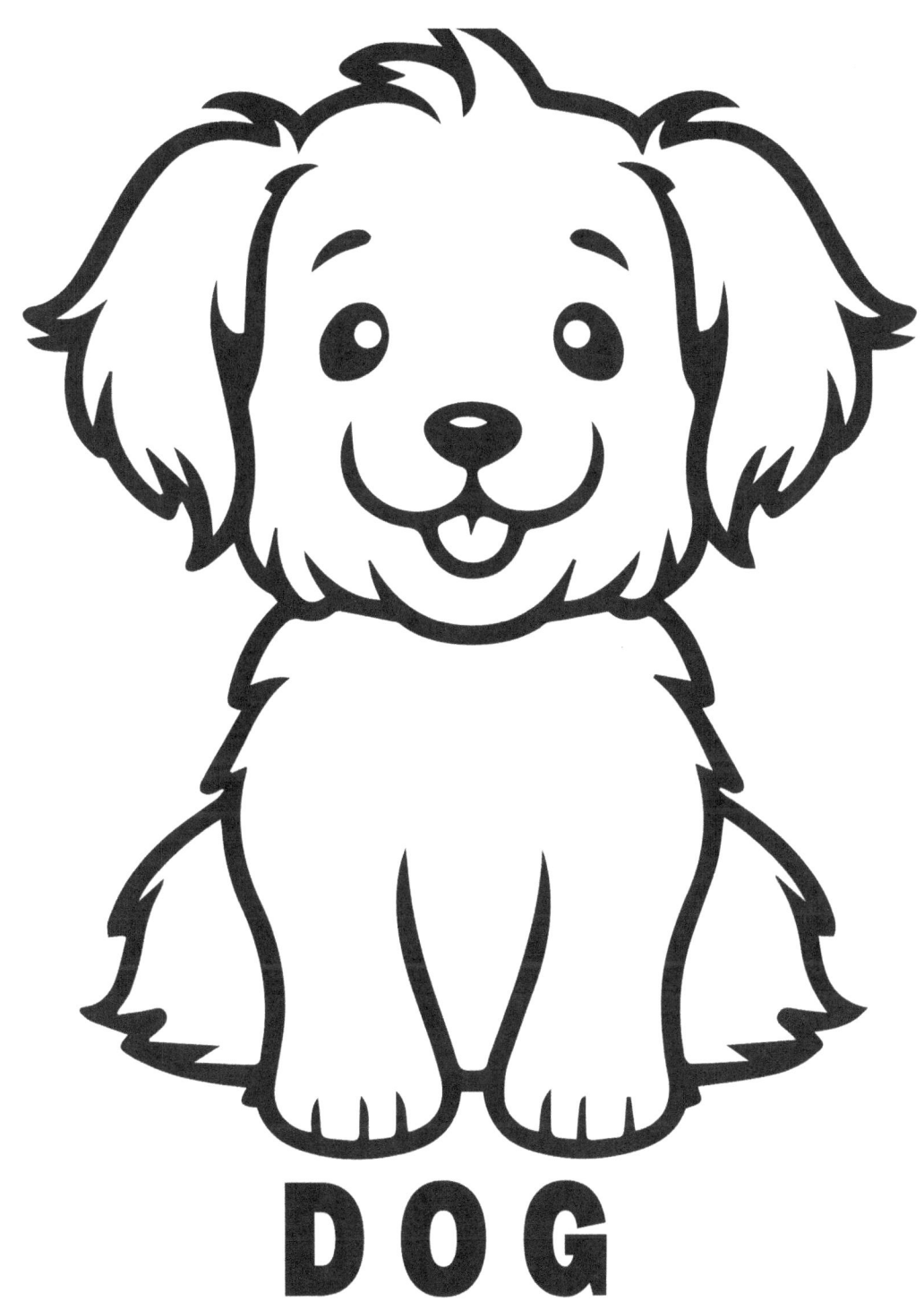

4. **DOG**

I'm a chirpy birdie who loves soaring high in the big blue sky!

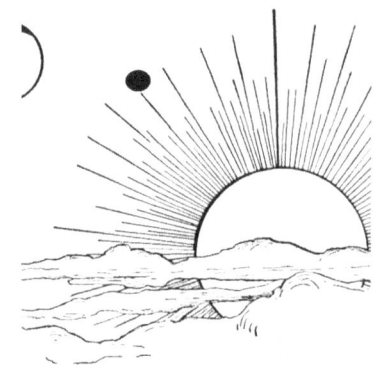

5.

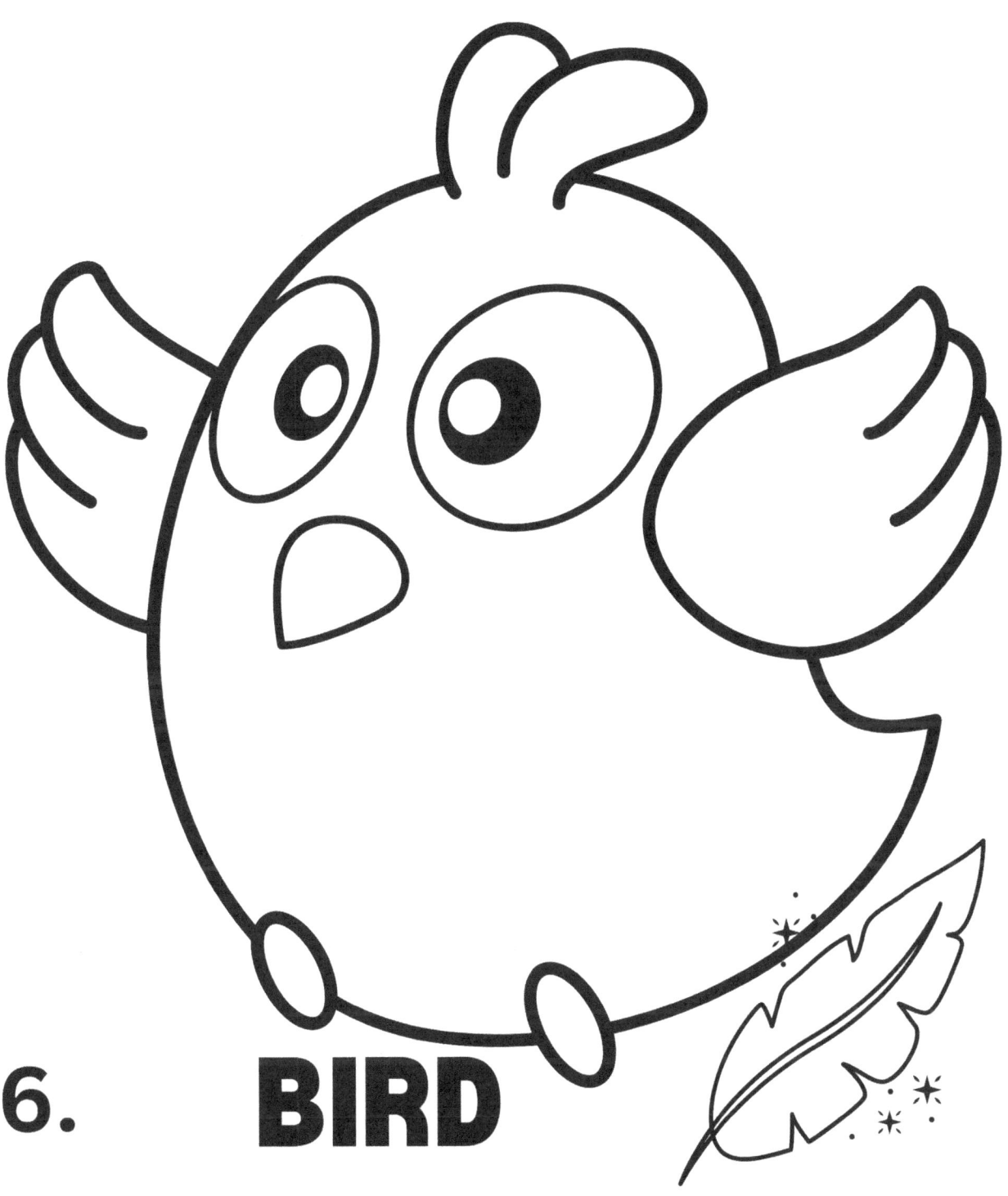

6. **BIRD**

I'm a happy horse who munches on hay all day and loves to gallop around in the fields with my friends!

7.

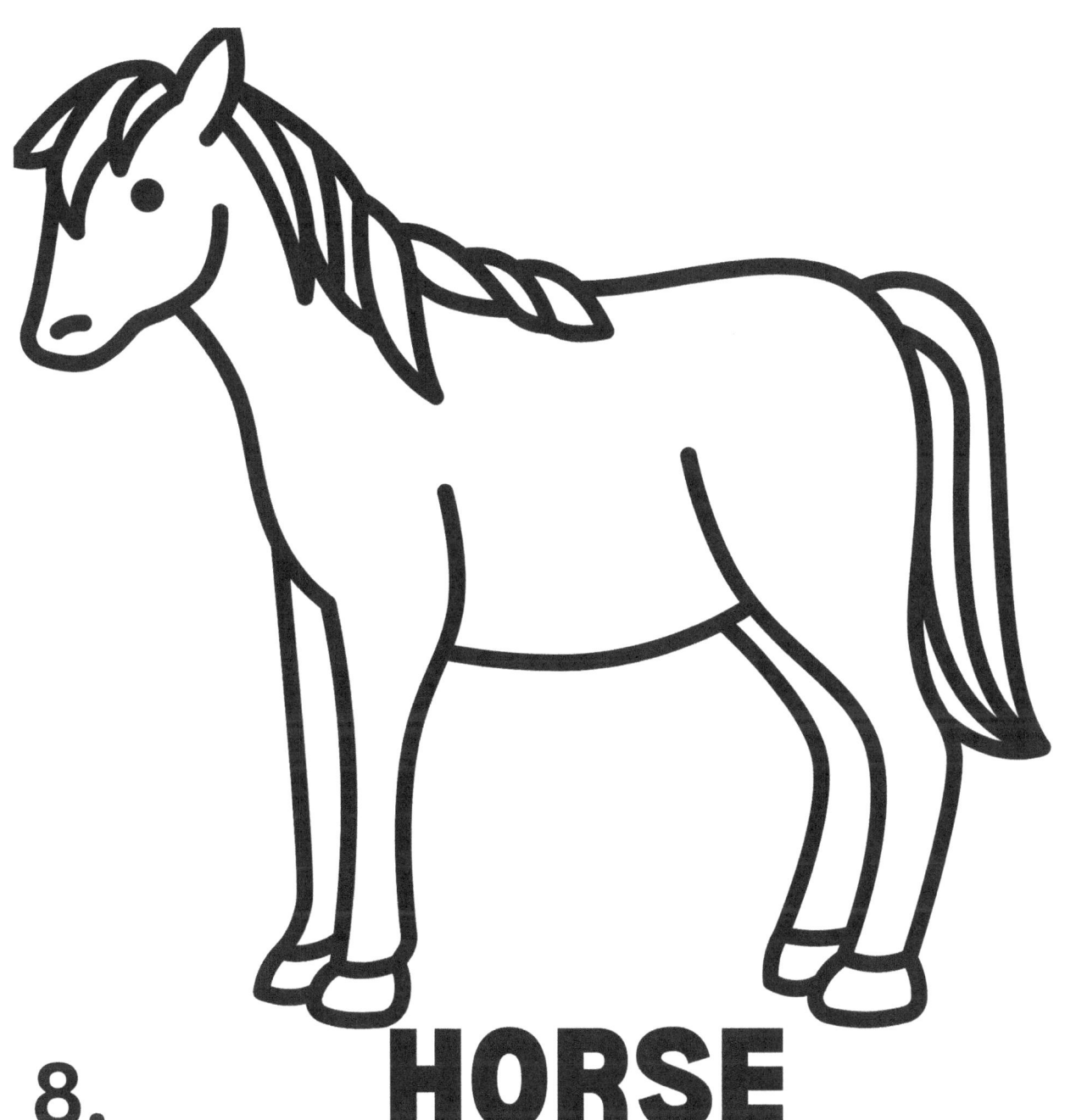

8. **HORSE**

I'm a cuddly bear who loves snuggling up in my cozy den for a long winter's nap!

9.

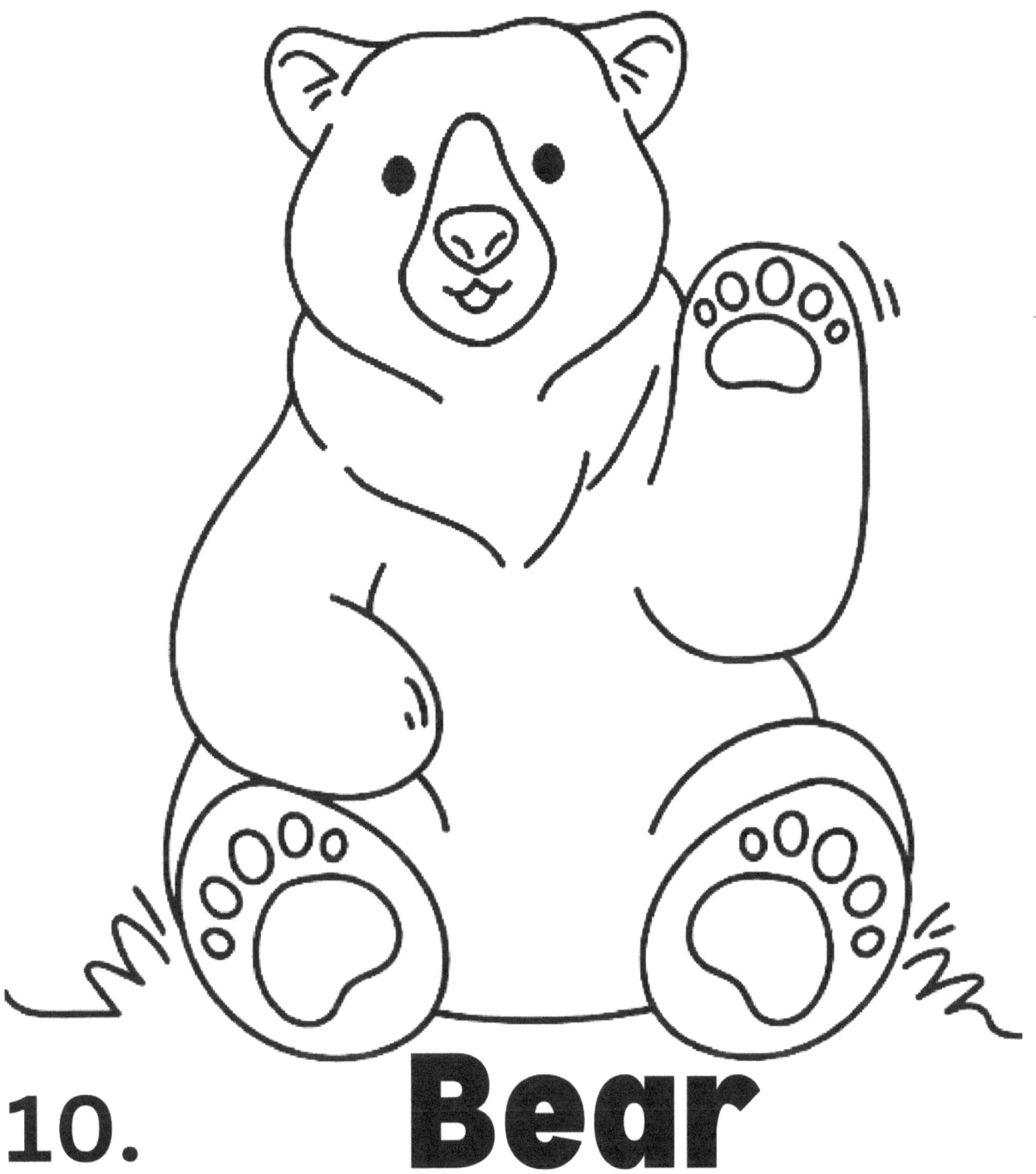

10. **Bear**

I'm a jumbo elephant who spends my days munching on tasty fruits and splashing around in the water for some fun!

11.

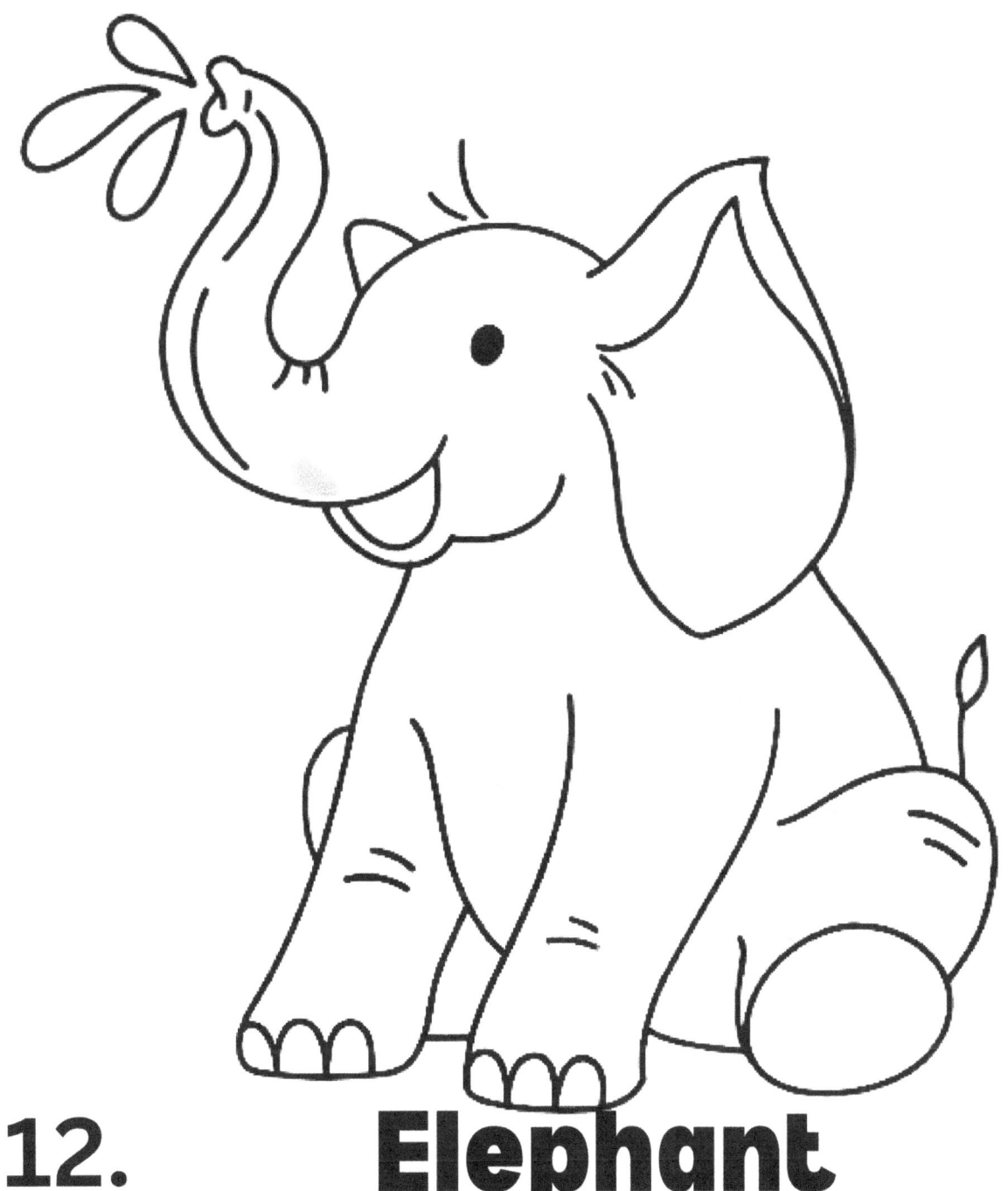

12. **Elephant**

"I'm a mischievous monkey who spends my days munching on yummy bananas and swinging from tree to tree, having a blast all the time!"

13.

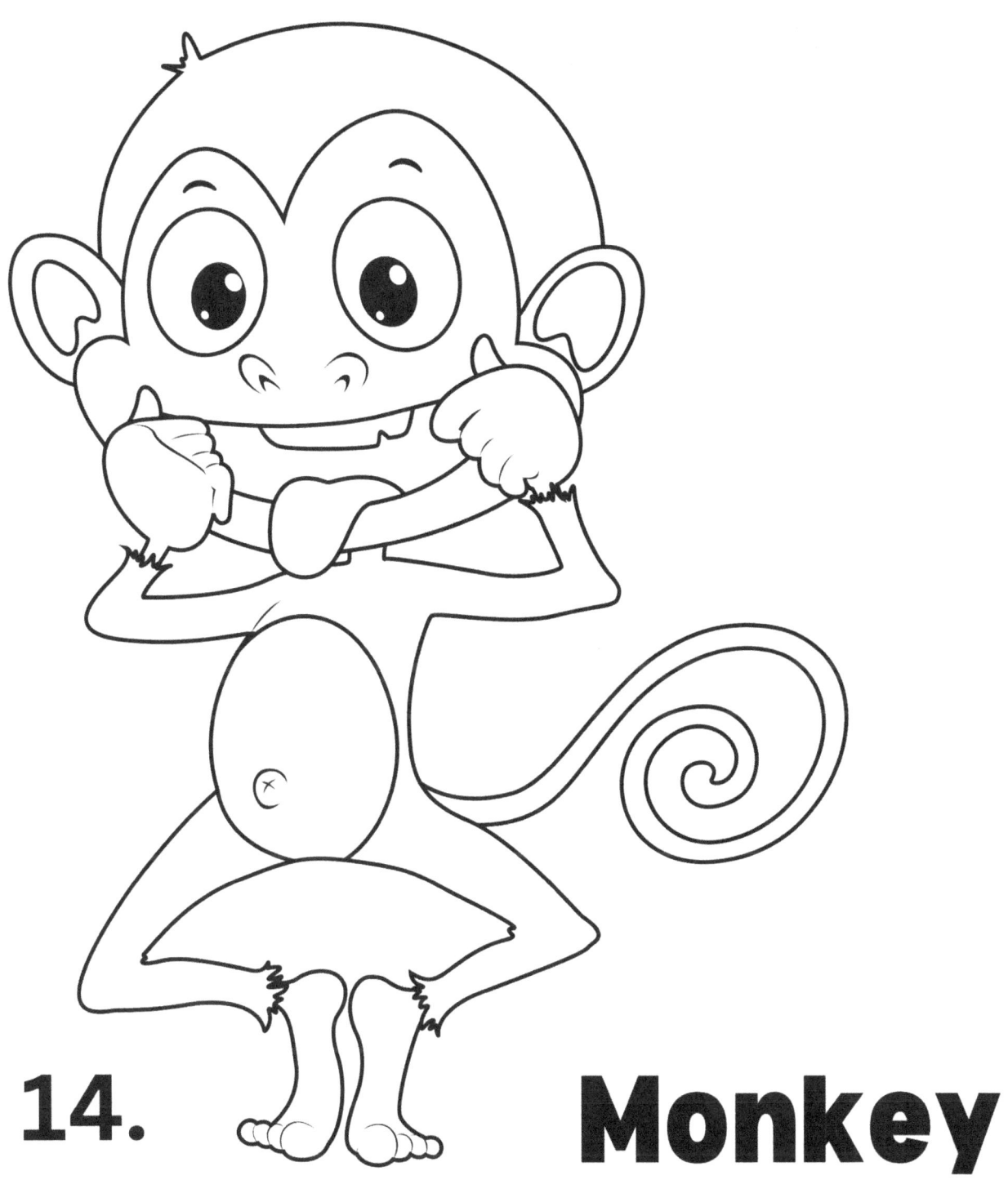

14. **Monkey**

"I'm a mighty rhinoceros, with my big horn and sturdy legs, stomping around and munching on tasty grass all day long.

15.

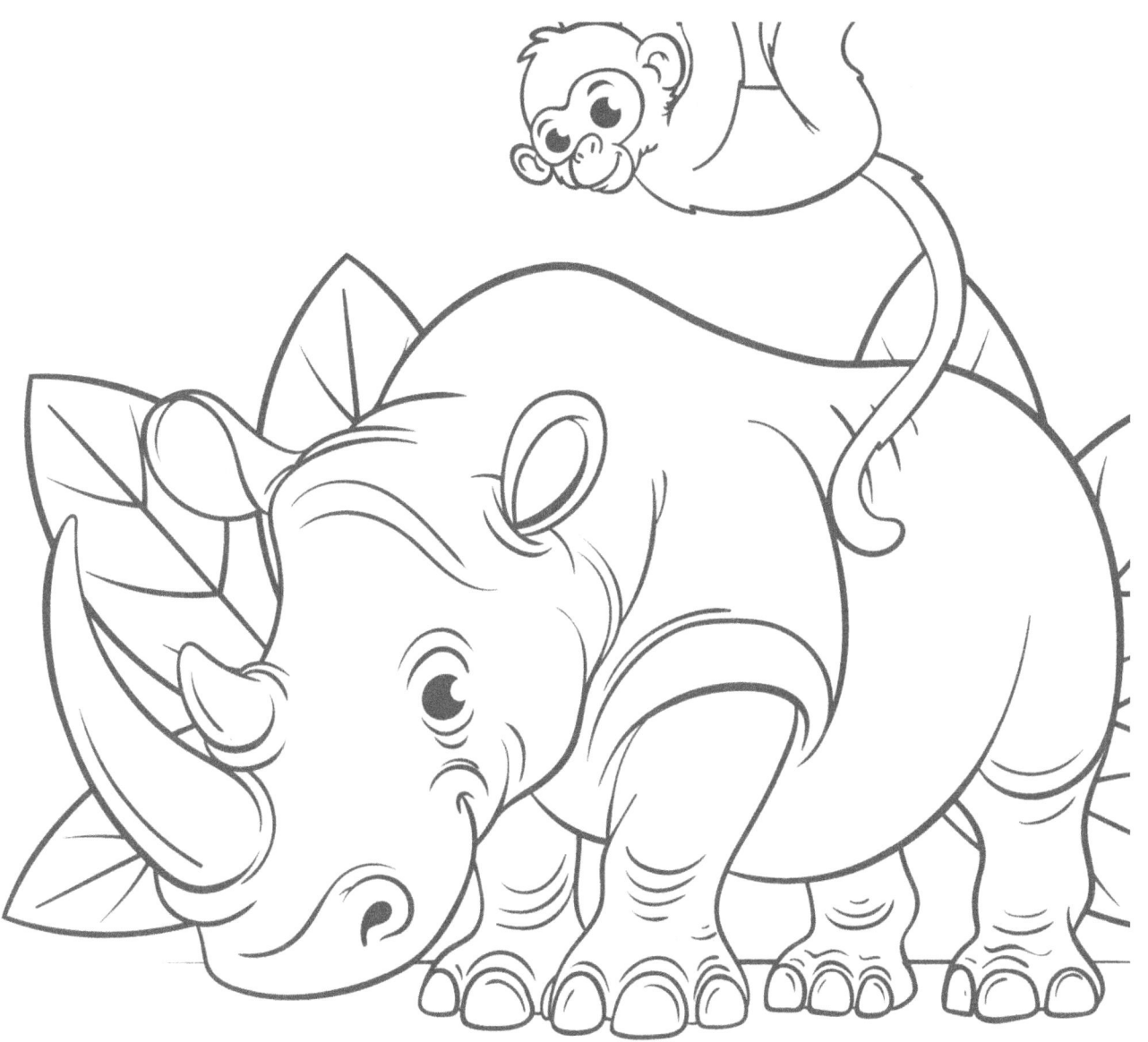

16. Rhinoceros

"I'm a sleek shark, gliding through the ocean with my powerful fins, and chomping on delicious fish all day long!"

17.

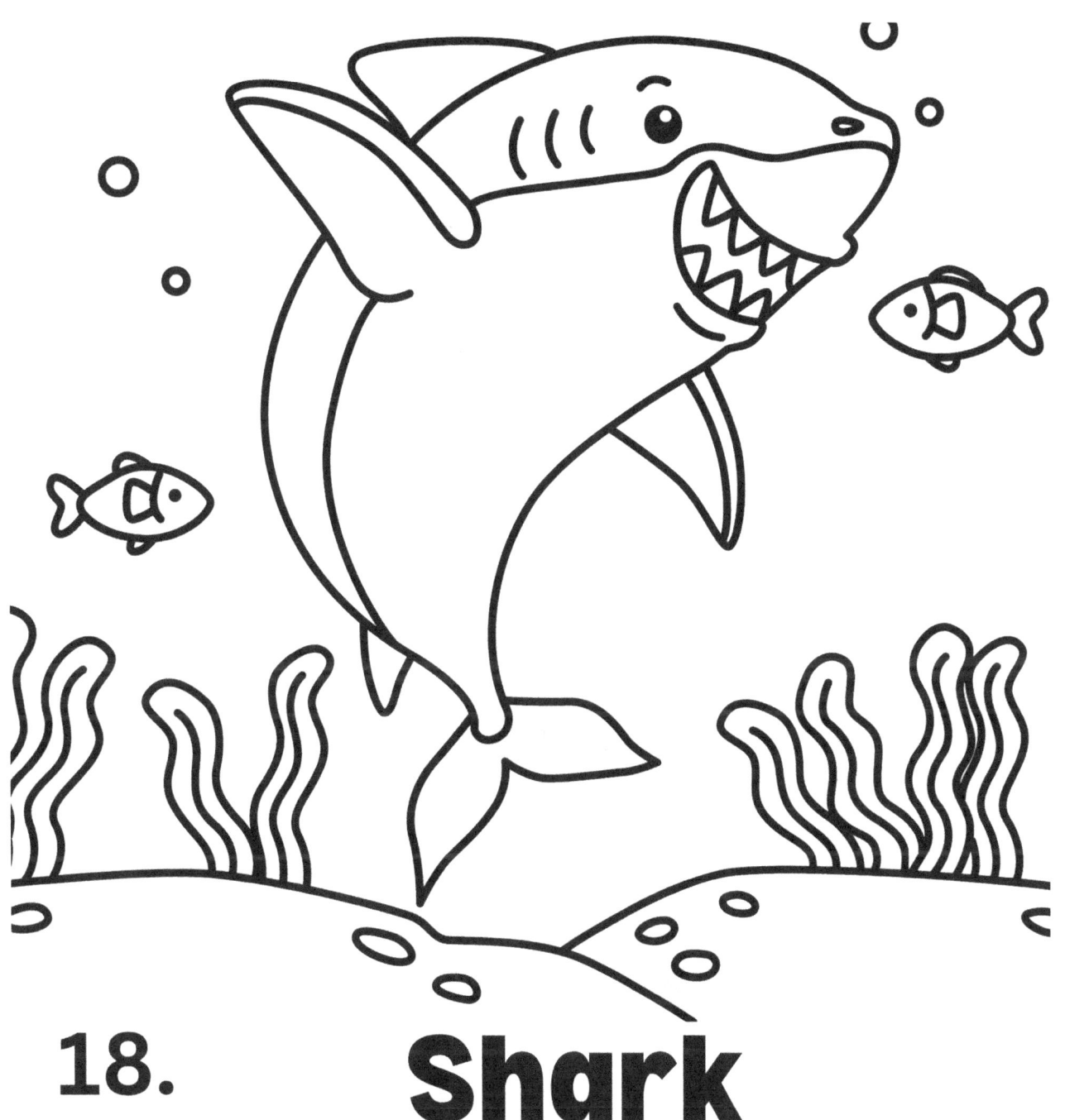

18. **Shark**

"I'm a playful dolphin, gliding through the ocean with my graceful fins, and gobbling up yummy fish all day long!

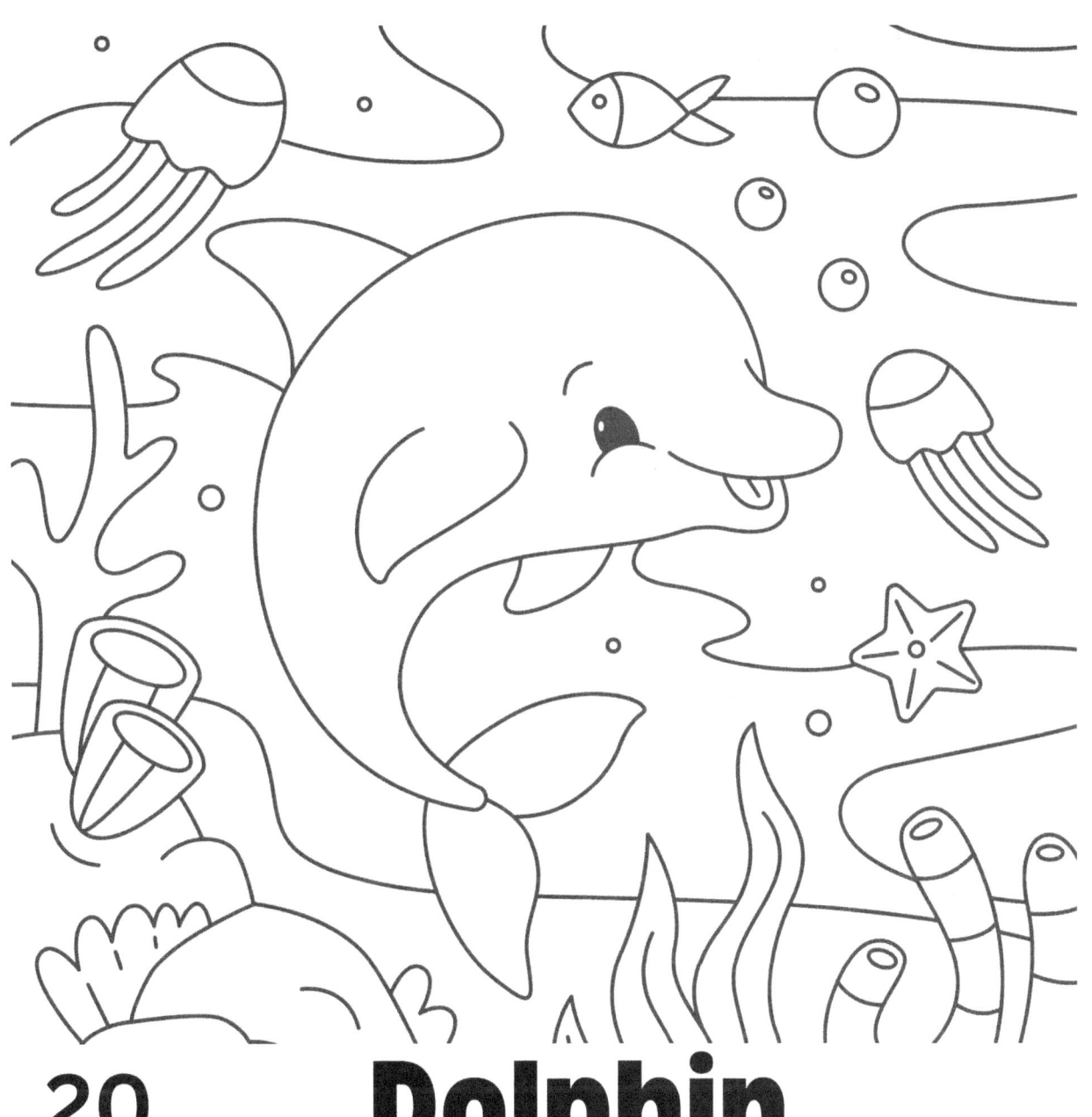

20. **Dolphin**

"I'm a clever fox, tiptoeing through the forest with my fluffy tail, and munching on tasty berries all day long!"

21.

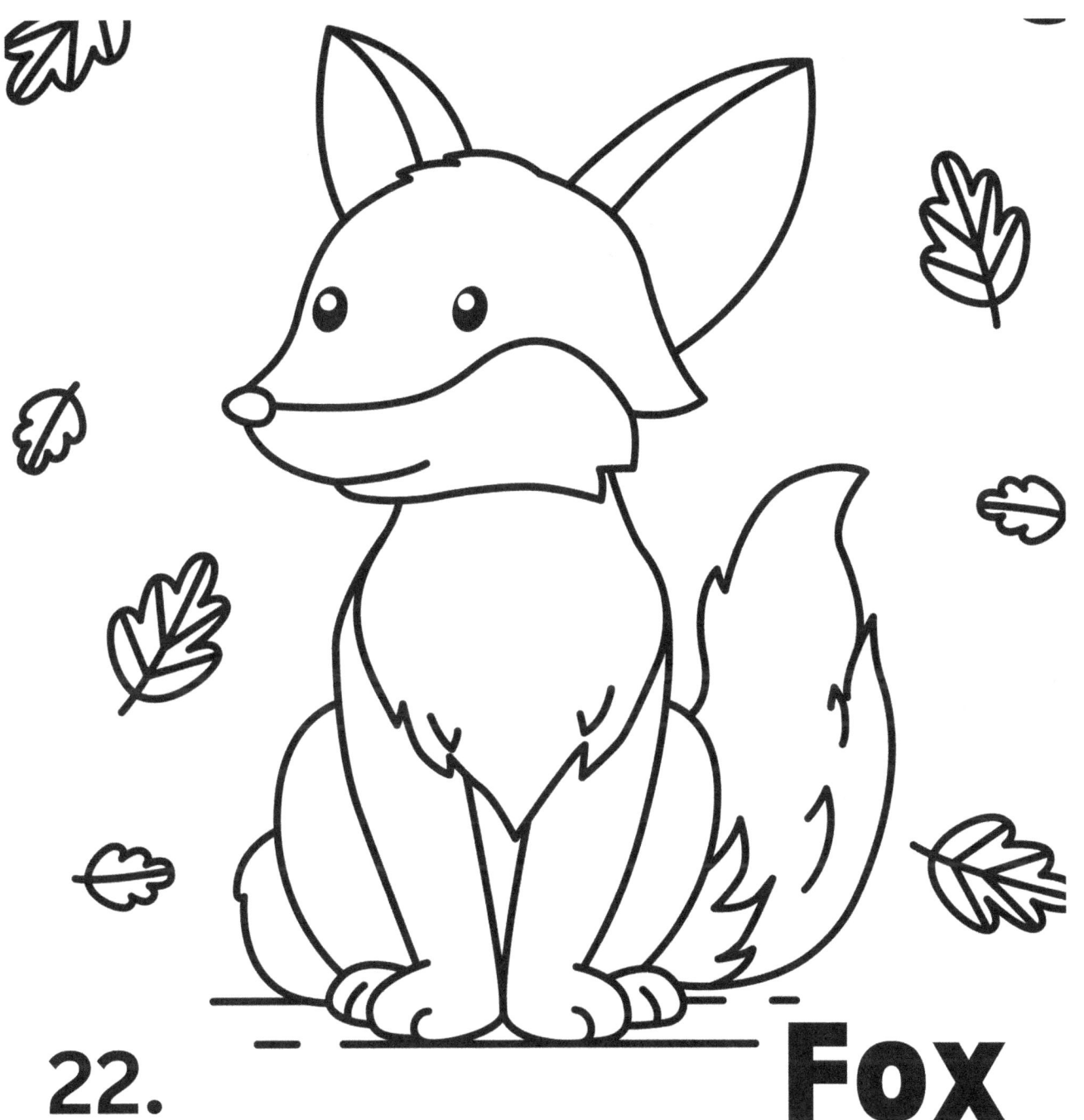

22. Fox

"I'm a wise turtle, strolling through the lush green fields with my shiny shell, and munching on delicious greens all day long.

23.

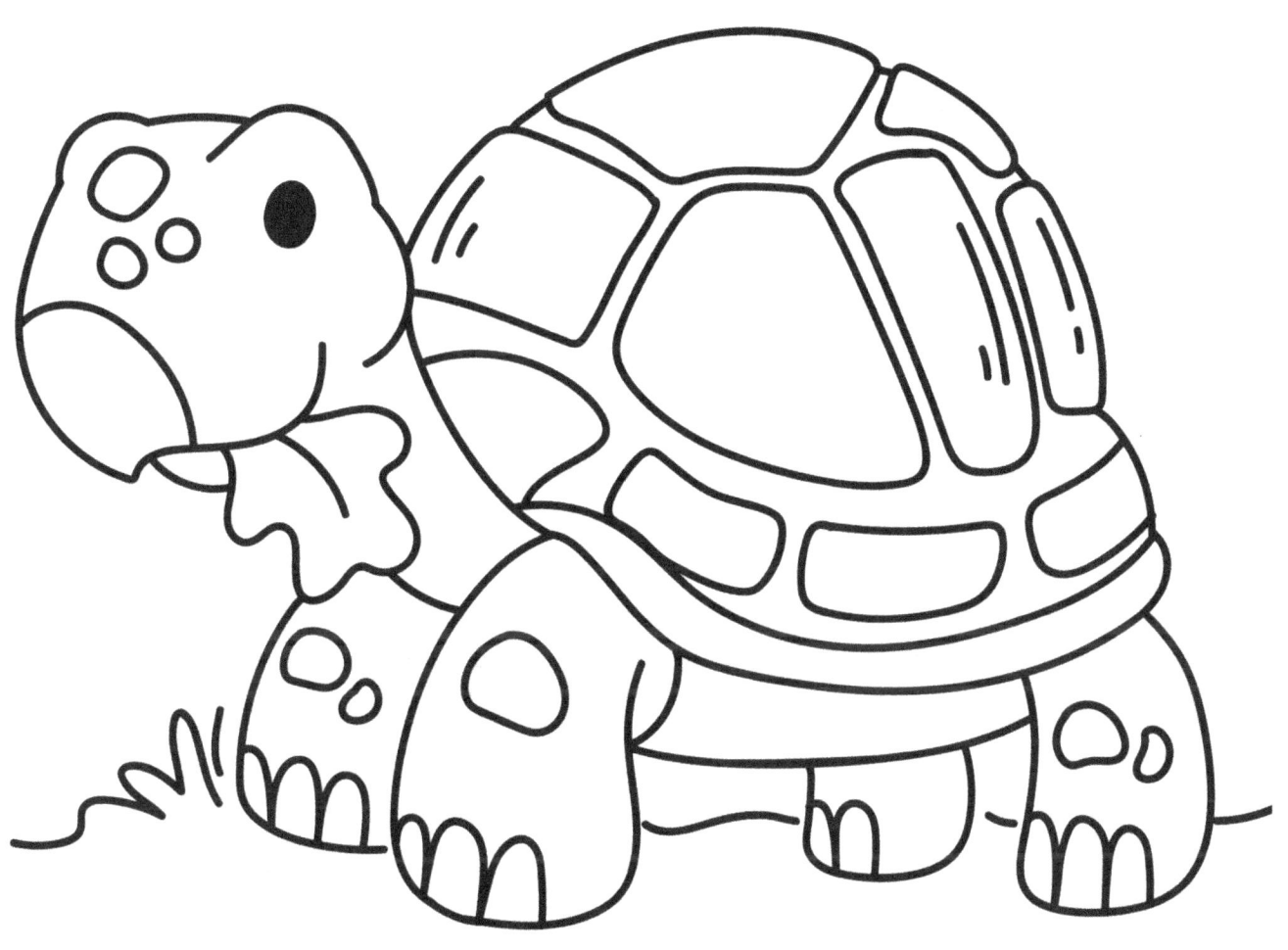

24. **Turtle**

"I'm a lively squirrel, darting through the trees with my bushy tail, and nibbling on tasty nuts all day long!"

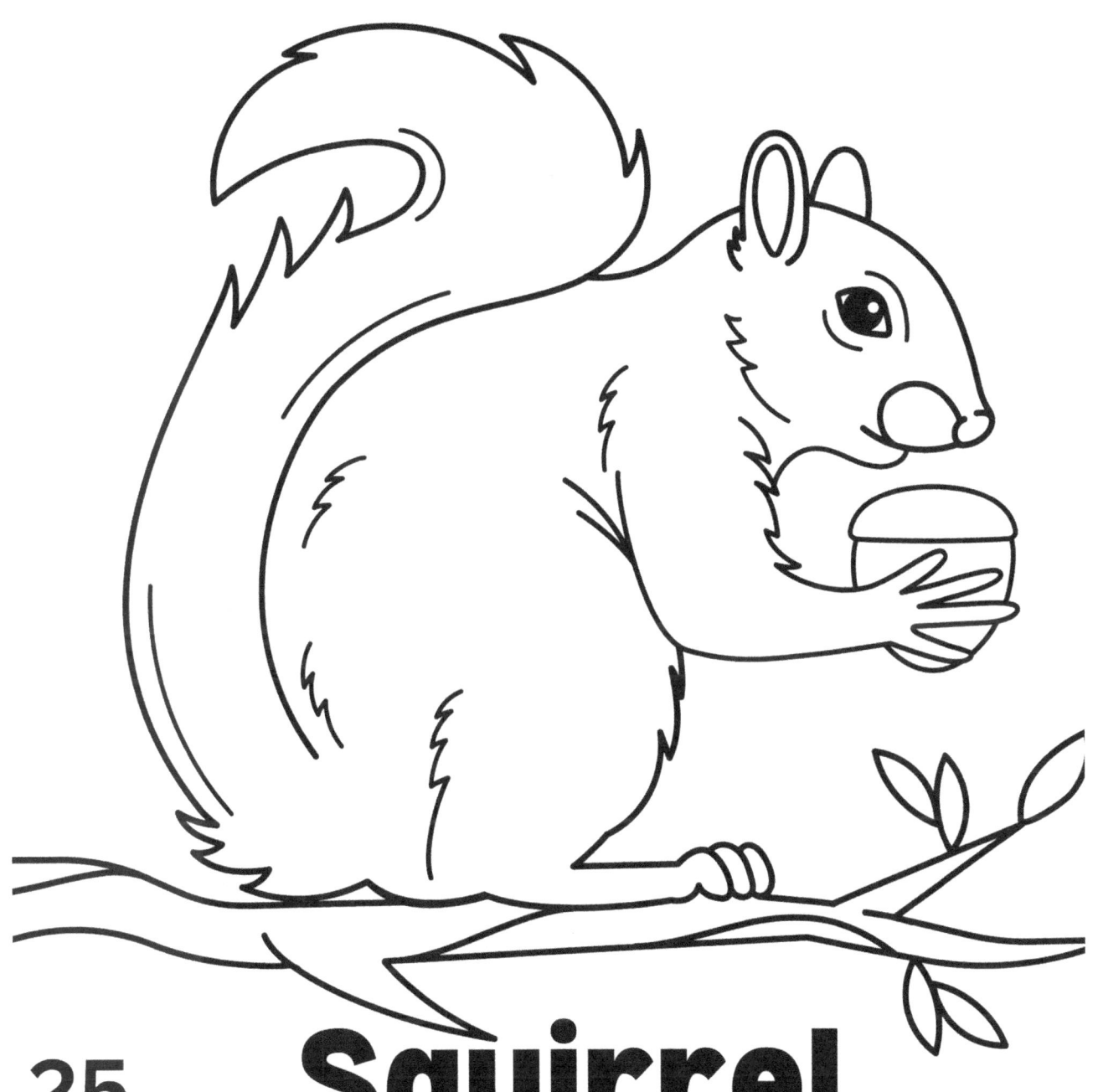

25. Squirrel

26. "I'm a mighty lion, roaming the savannah with my golden mane, and roaring to let everyone know who's king of the jungle!"

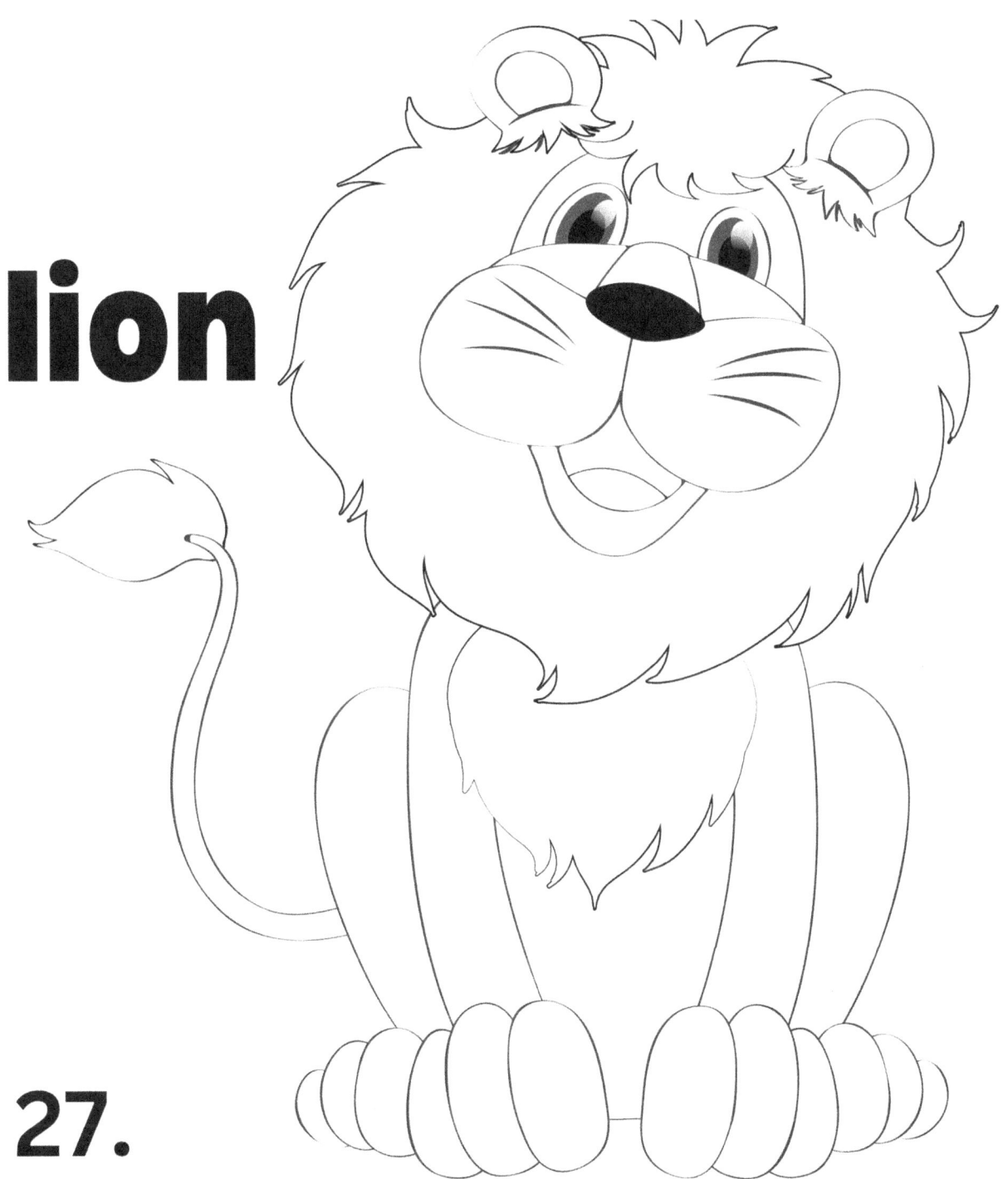

lion

27.

28. "I'm a fierce T-Rex, stomping through the ancient forests with my massive jaws, and roaring to show who's the boss of the prehistoric (uf) world!"

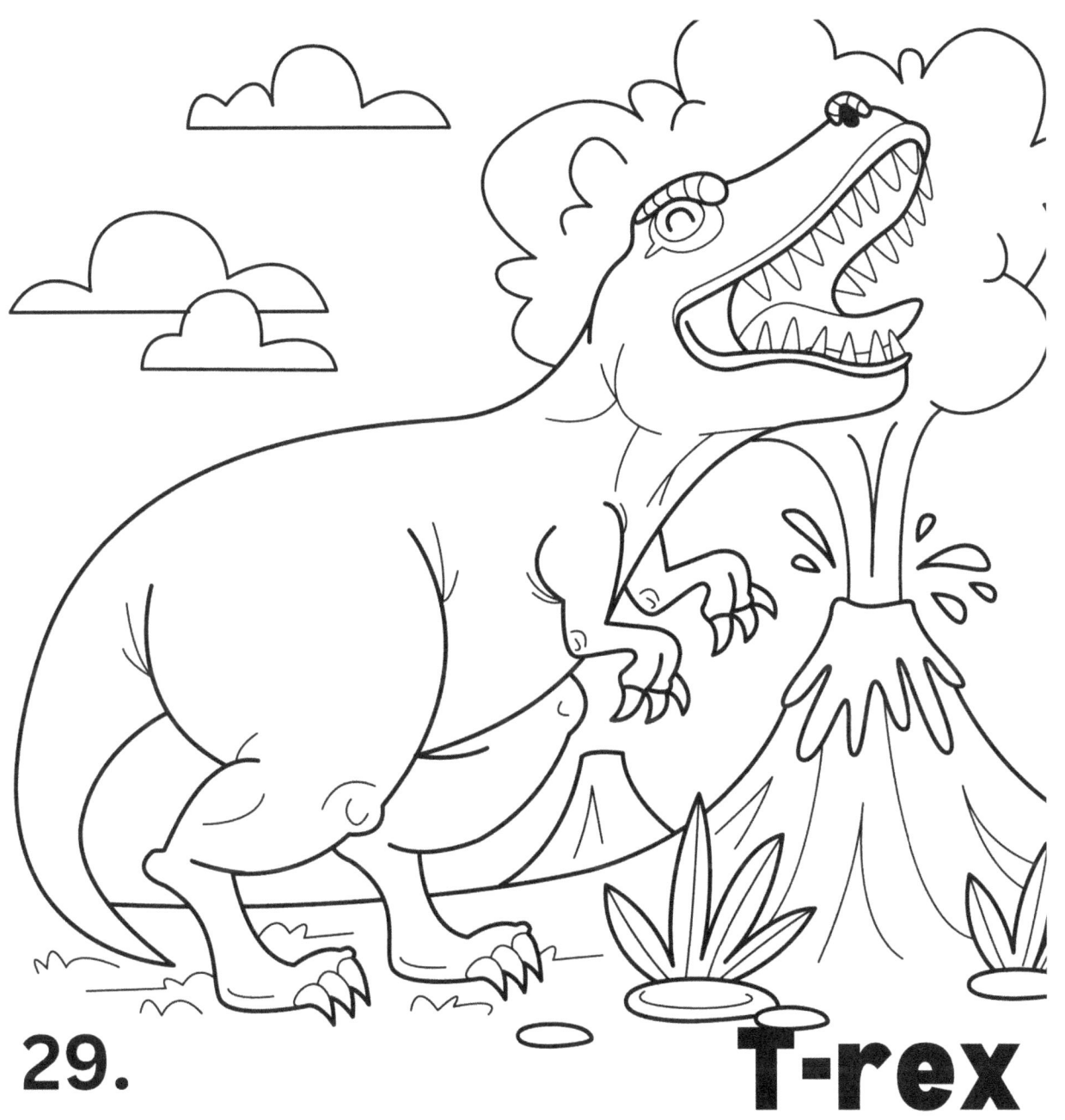

29. T-rex

30. "I'm a sleek tiger, prowling through the jungle with my stripes, and pouncing on prey with a mighty roar!"

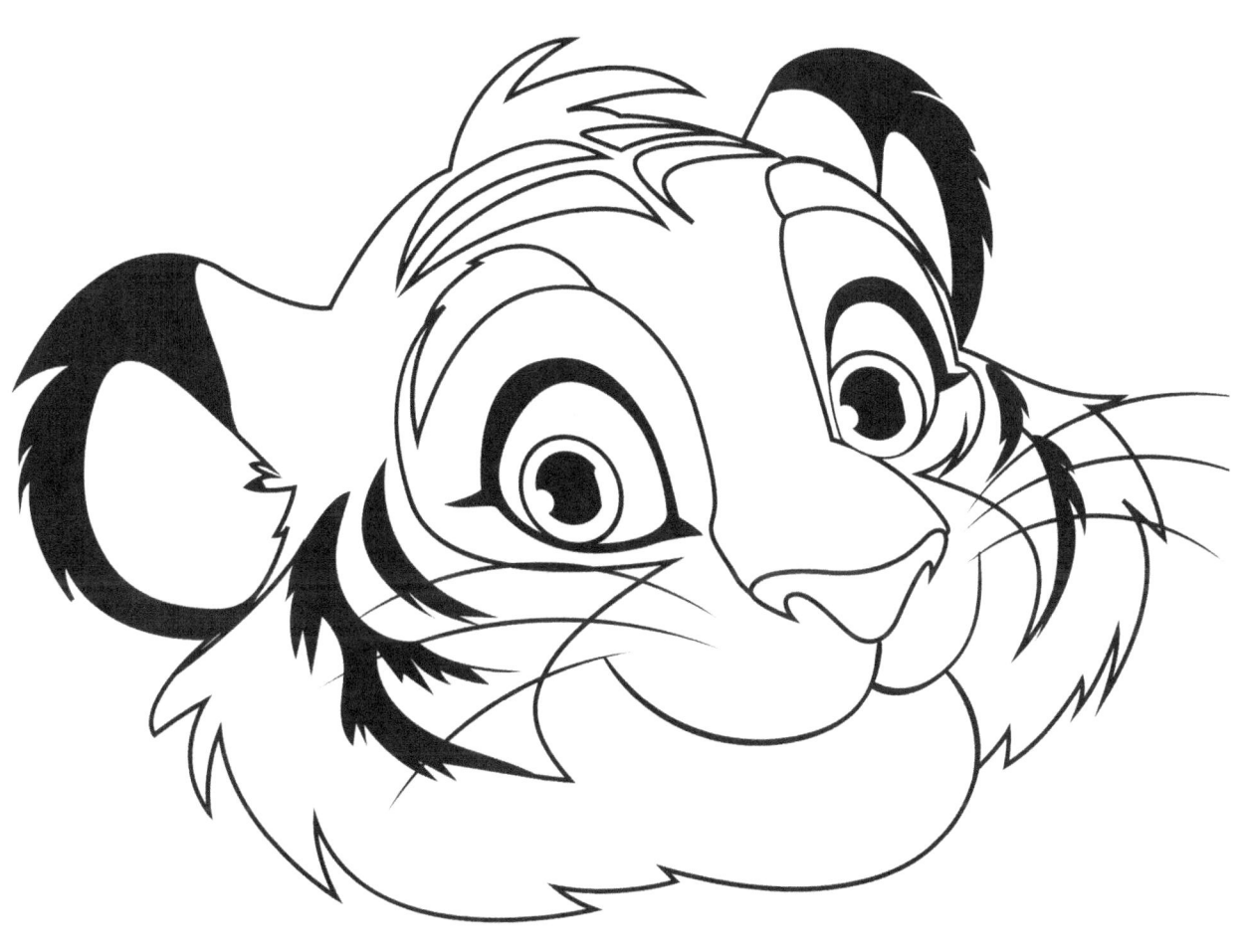

30. **Tiger**

"I'm a tiny mouse, scurrying through the cozy burrows with my twitchy whiskers, and nibbling on delicious cheese whenever I can find it!"

31.

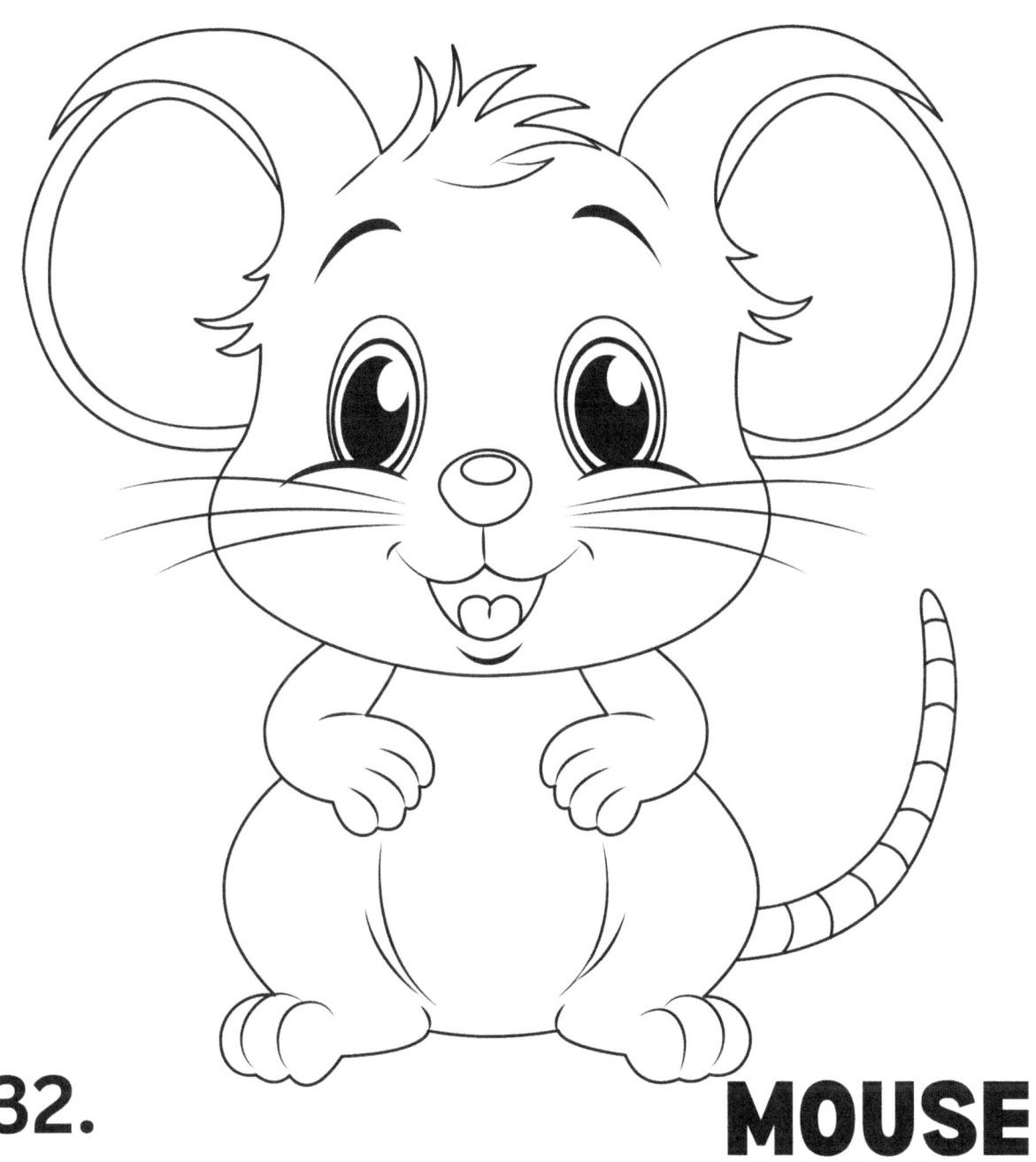

32. MOUSE

"I'm a fluffy chicken, strutting around the farmyard with my feathery friends, clucking and pecking at yummy grains all day long!"

33.

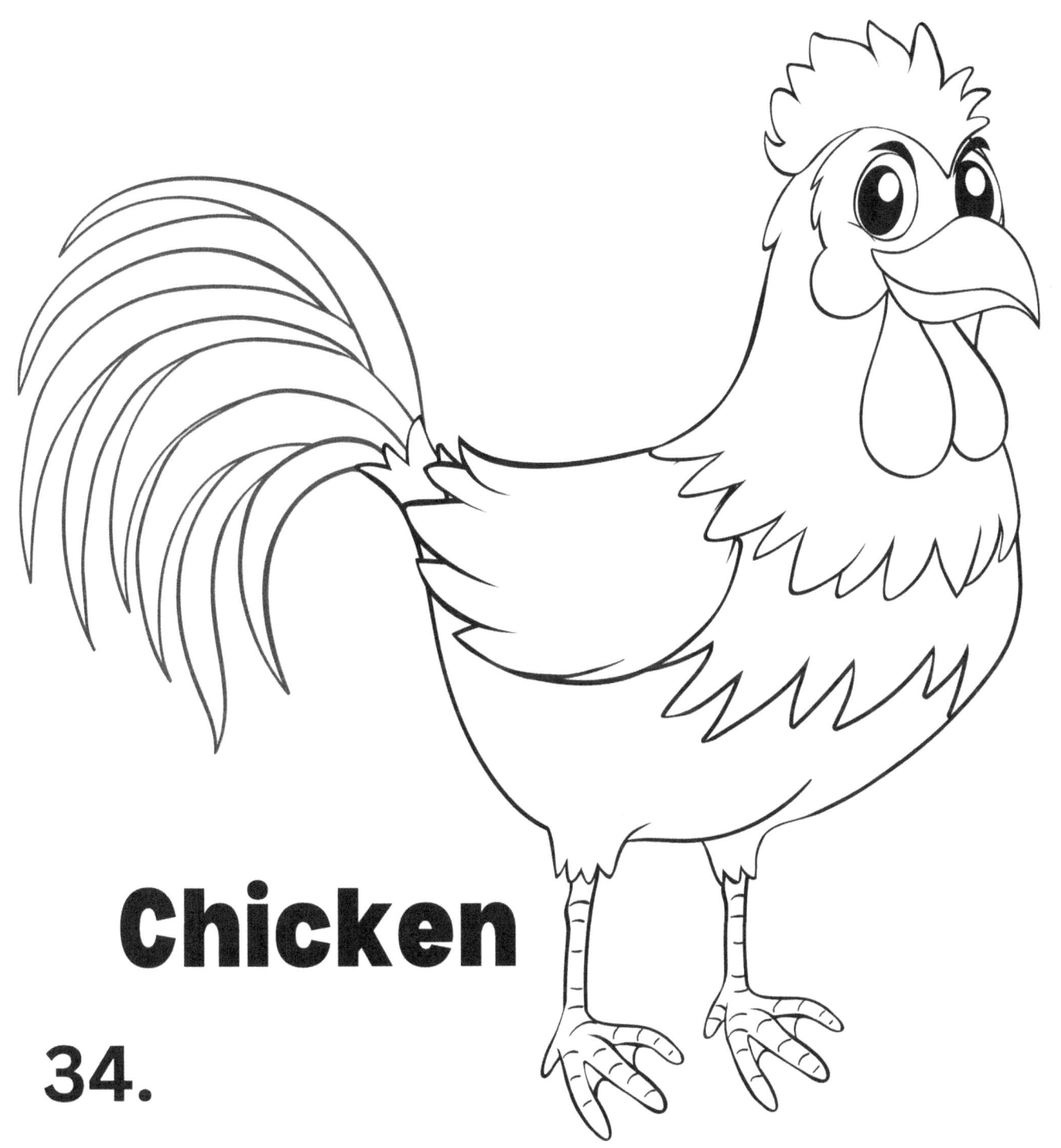

Chicken

34.

"I'm a gentle cow, mooing in the green pastures with my swishing tail, happily munching on sweet grass and dreaming of sunny days!

35.

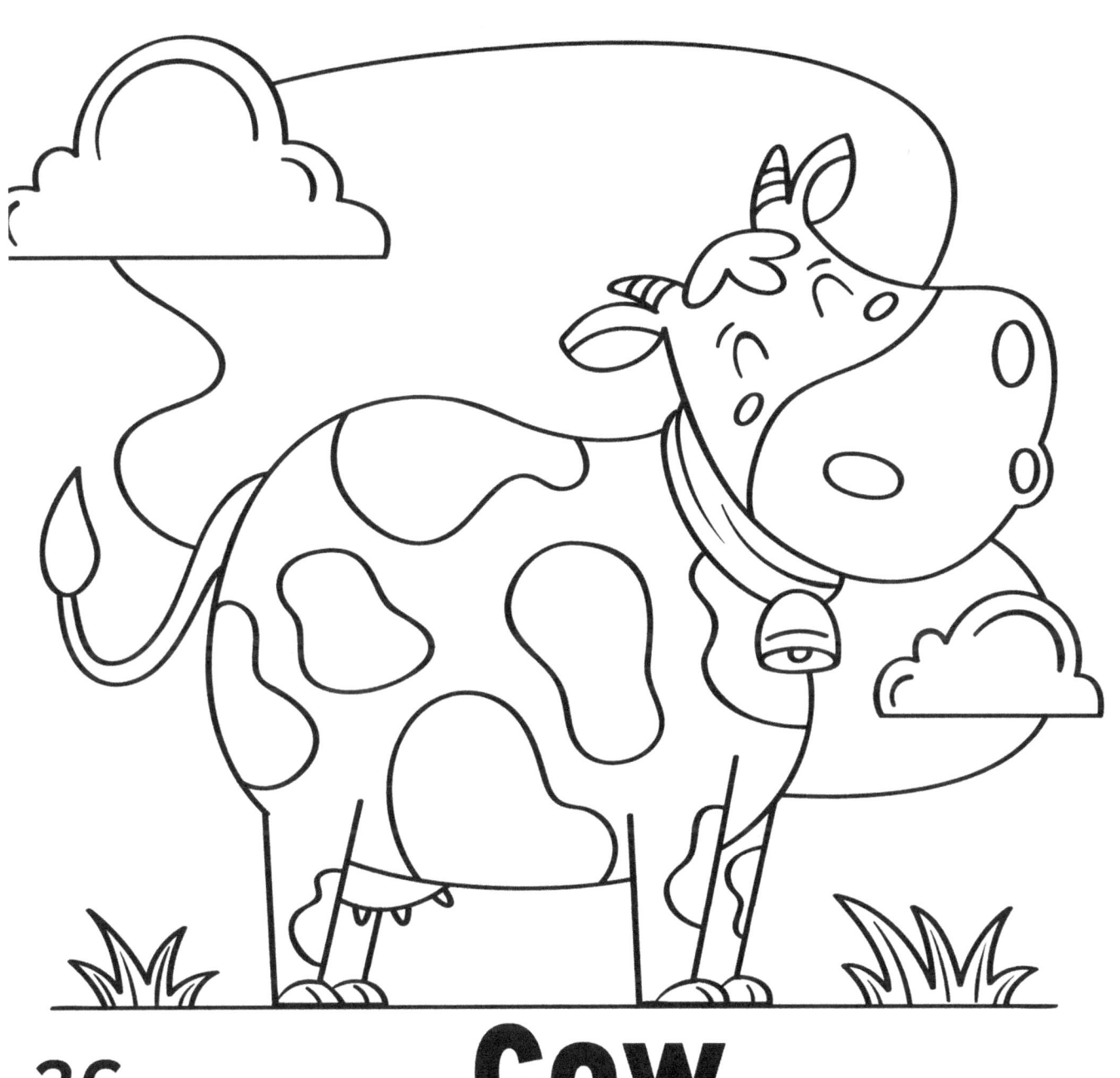

36. **Cow**

"I'm a graceful giraffe, strolling through the savannah with my long neck, and munching on leaves from the tallest trees like a leafy snack!"

37.

Giraffe

38.

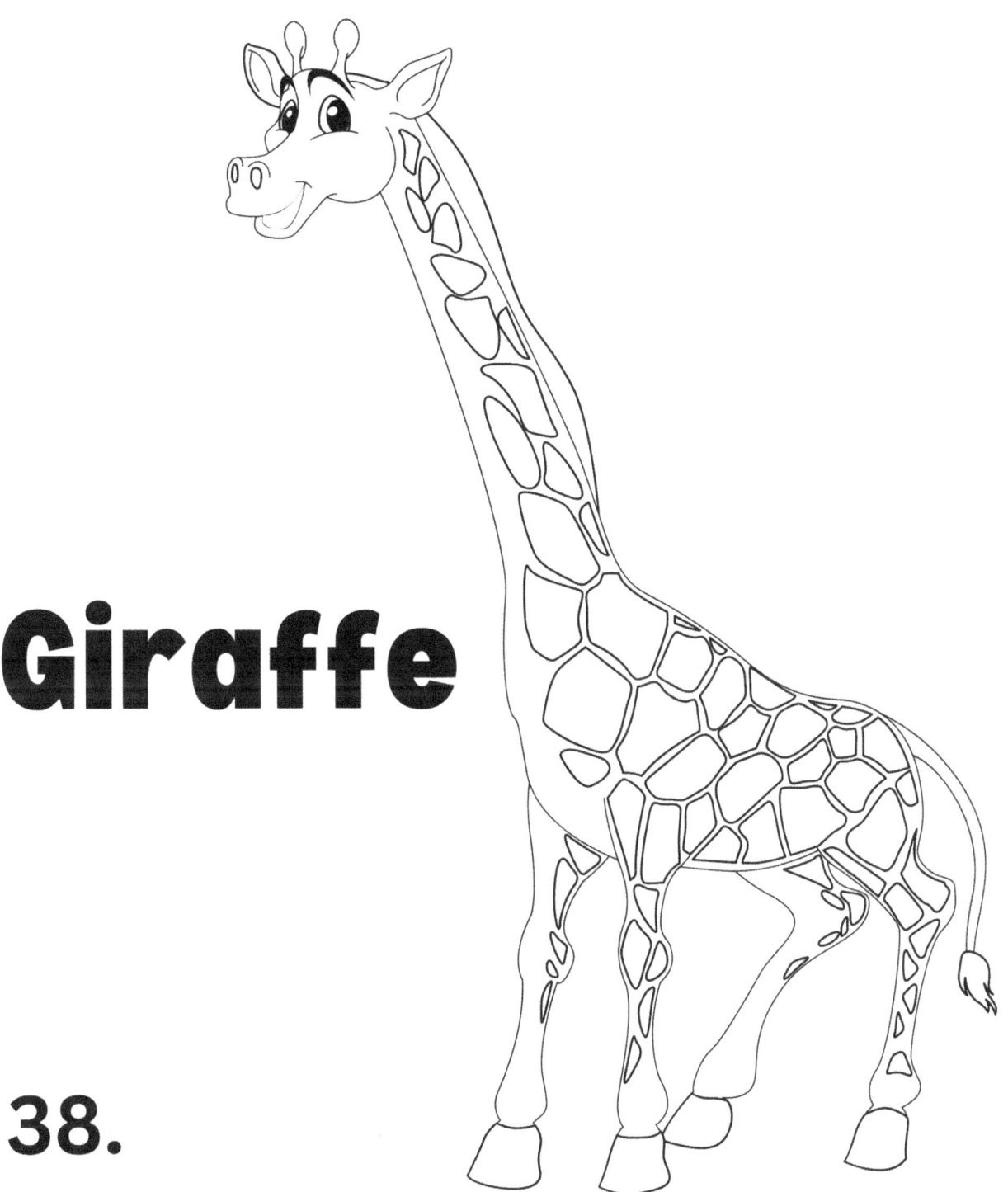

"I'm a hoppy rabbit, bouncing through the meadows with my twitchy nose, nibbling on crisp carrots and exploring every cozy burrow I find!"

39.

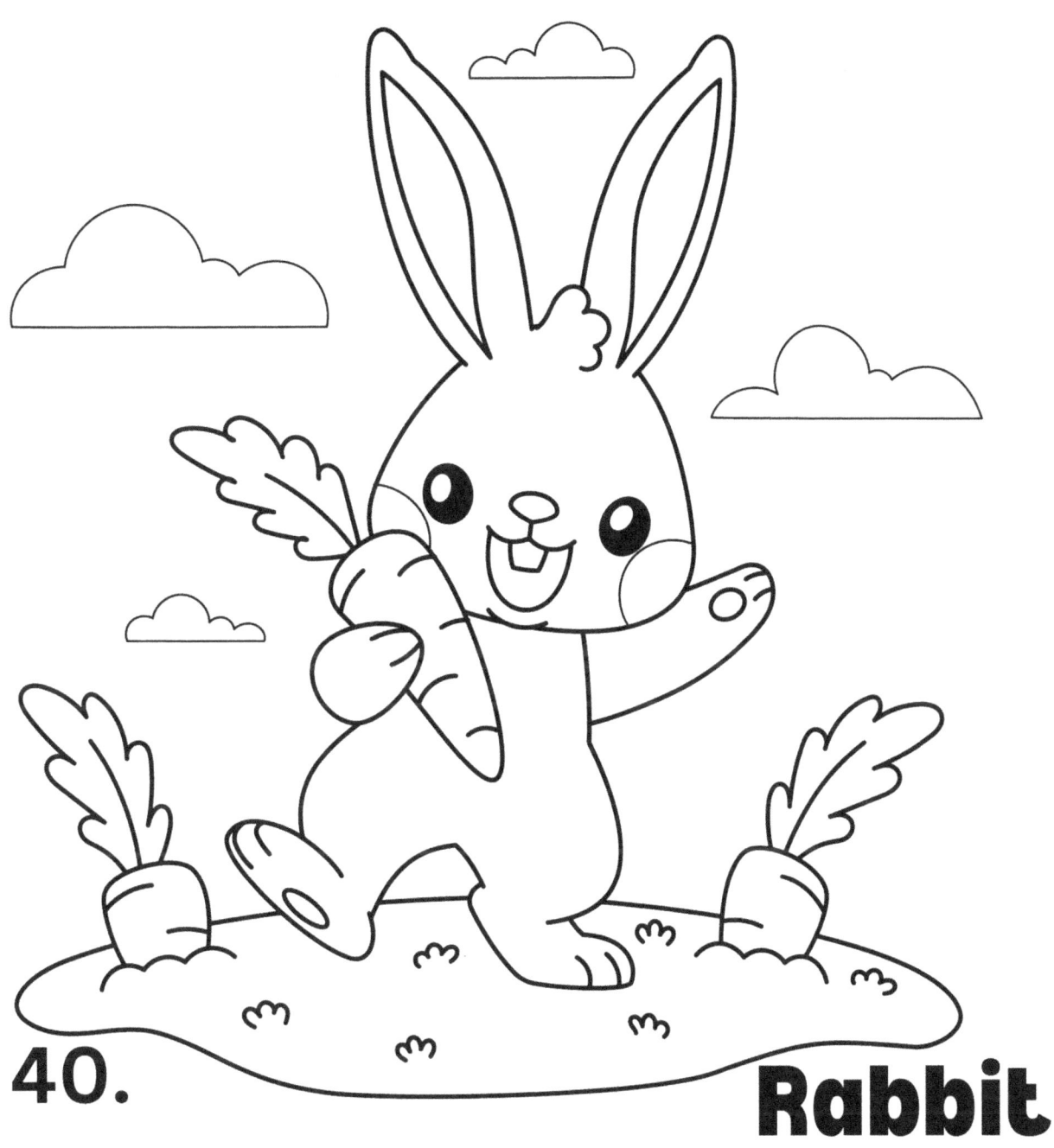

40. **Rabbit**

"I'm a leaping frog, hopping around the pond with my big, bulging eyes, croaking tunes with my froggy friends and catching tasty flies for dinner!"

41.

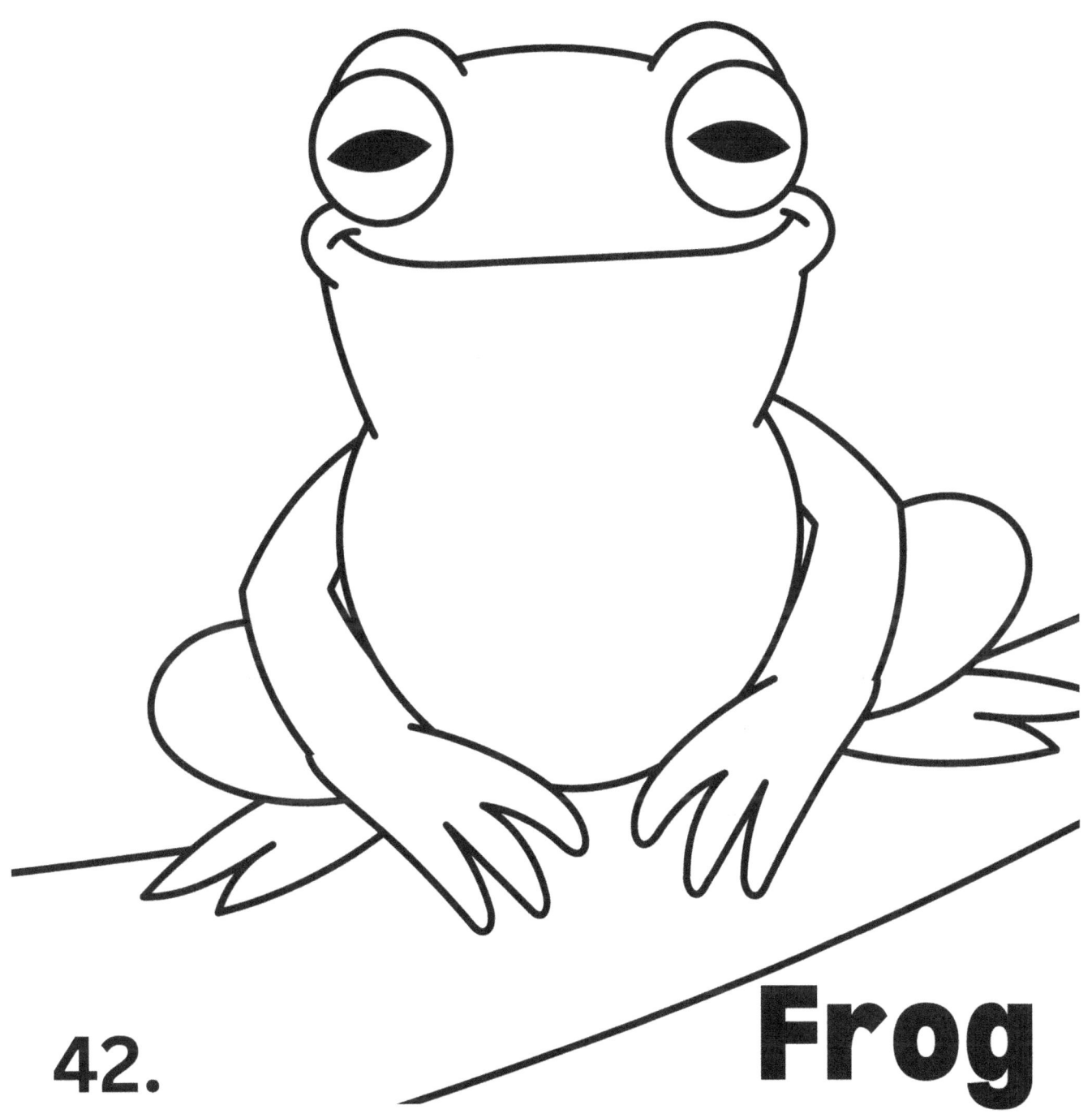

42.

Frog

"I'm a colorful parrot, perching in the treetops with my vibrant feathers, squawking and mimicking all the sounds I hear, from the chirping of birds to the laughter of children!"

43.

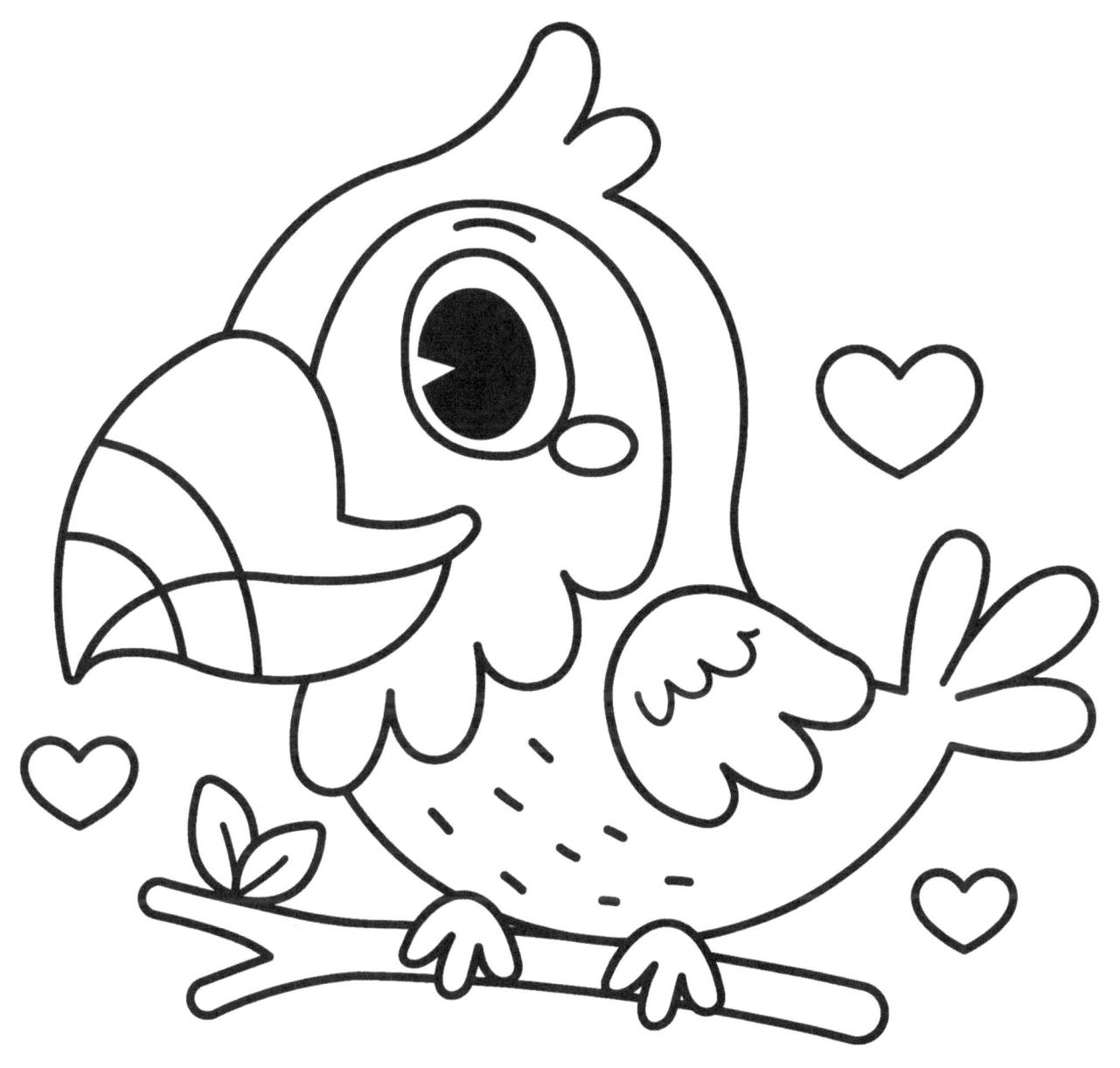

44.

Parrot

"I'm a sideways scuttling crab, exploring the sandy shores with my pincers snapping, searching for tasty treats hidden beneath the waves!"

45.

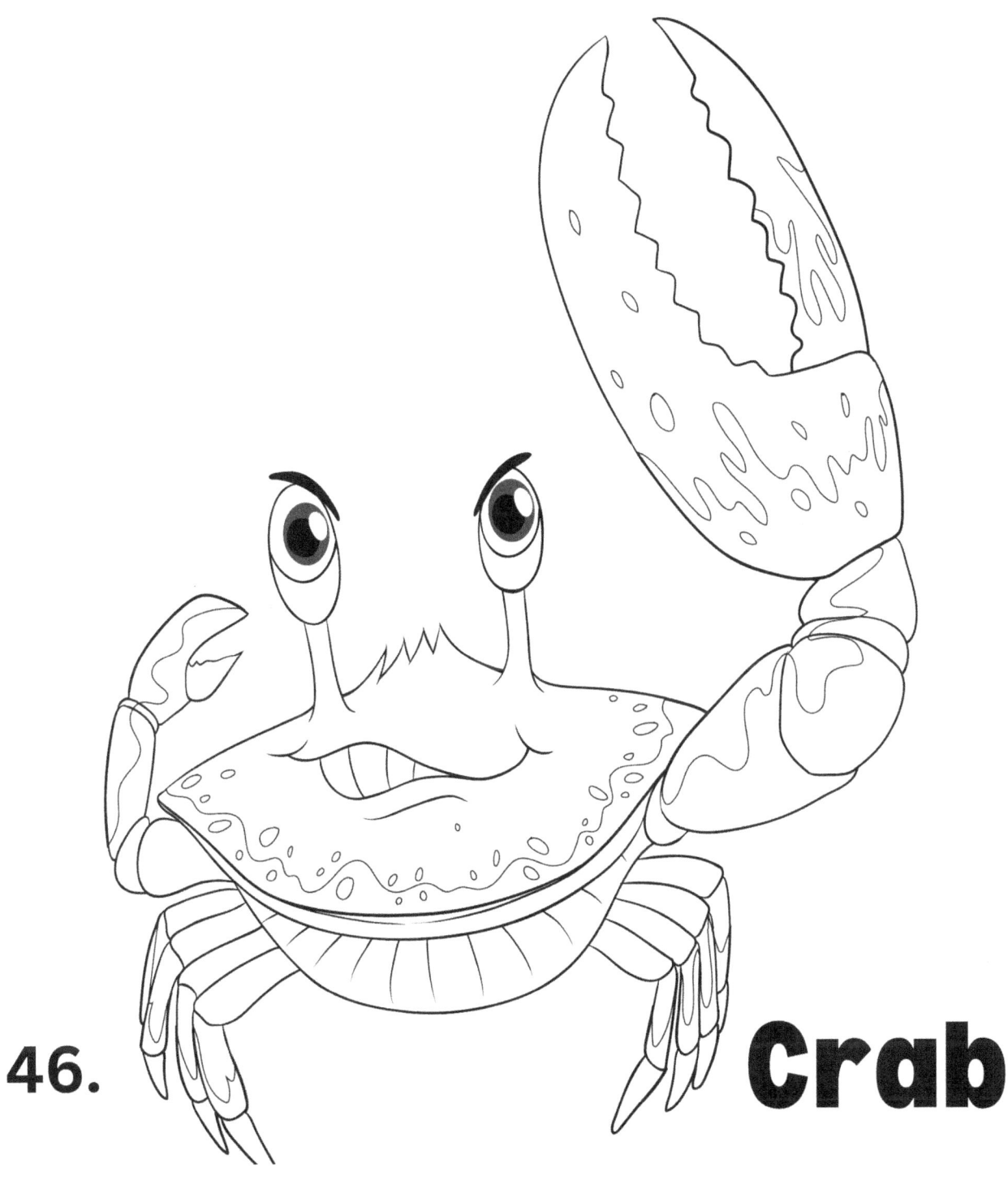

46. Crab

"I'm a magical reindeer, prancing through the snowy forests with my jingling bells, spreading joy and delivering gifts with Santa Claus on 47. Christmas Eve!"

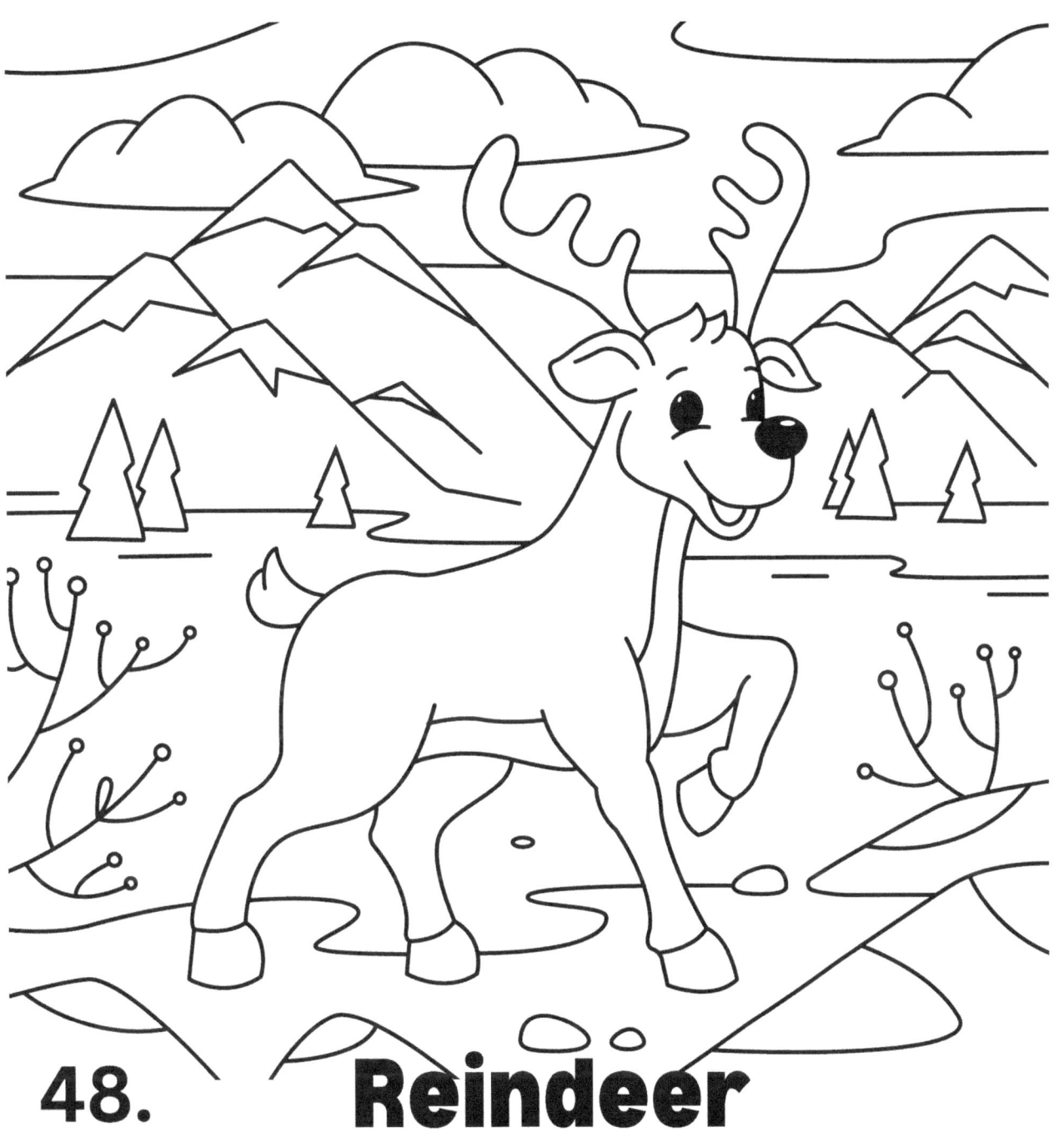

48. **Reindeer**

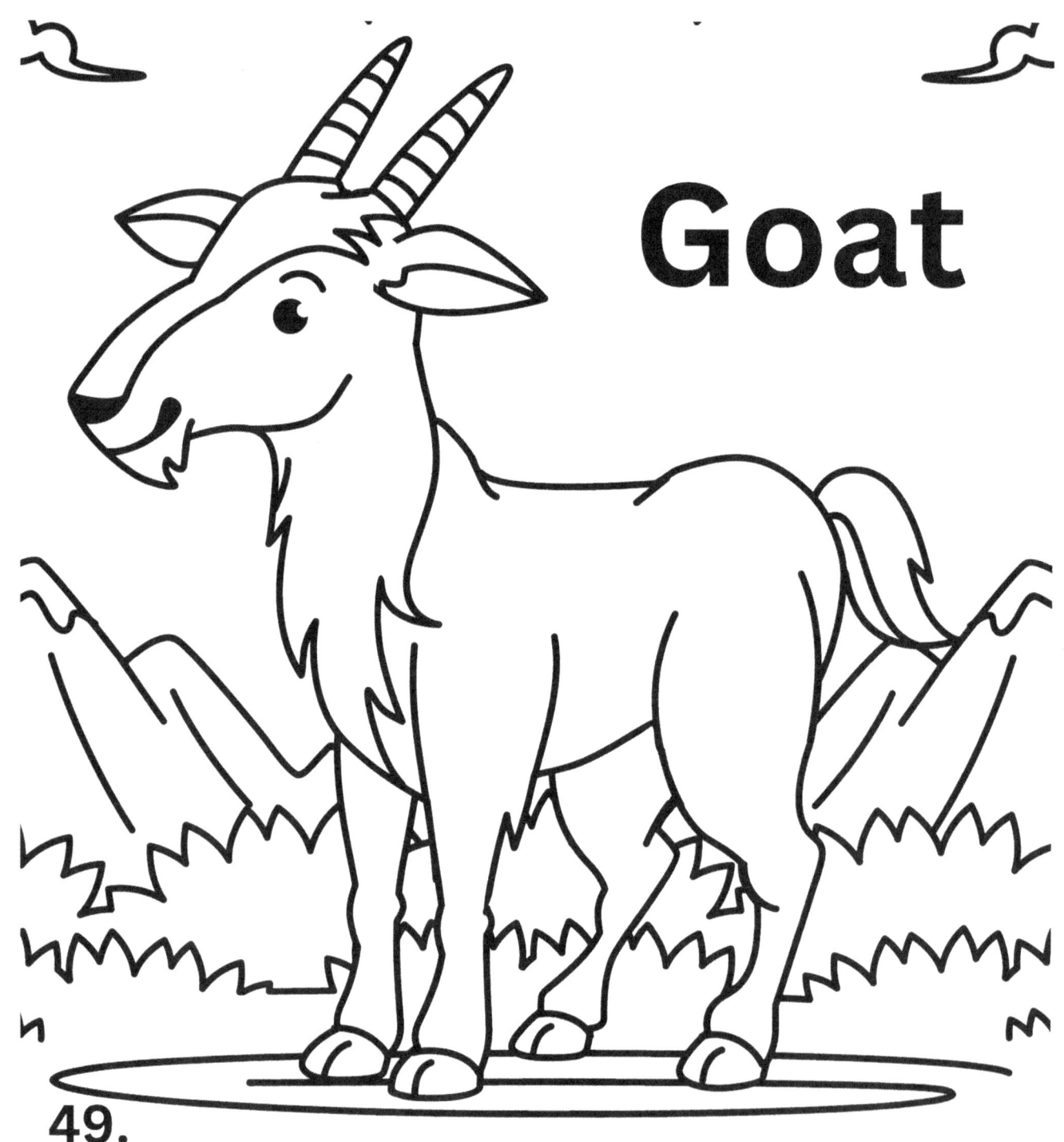

Goat

49.

Puppies

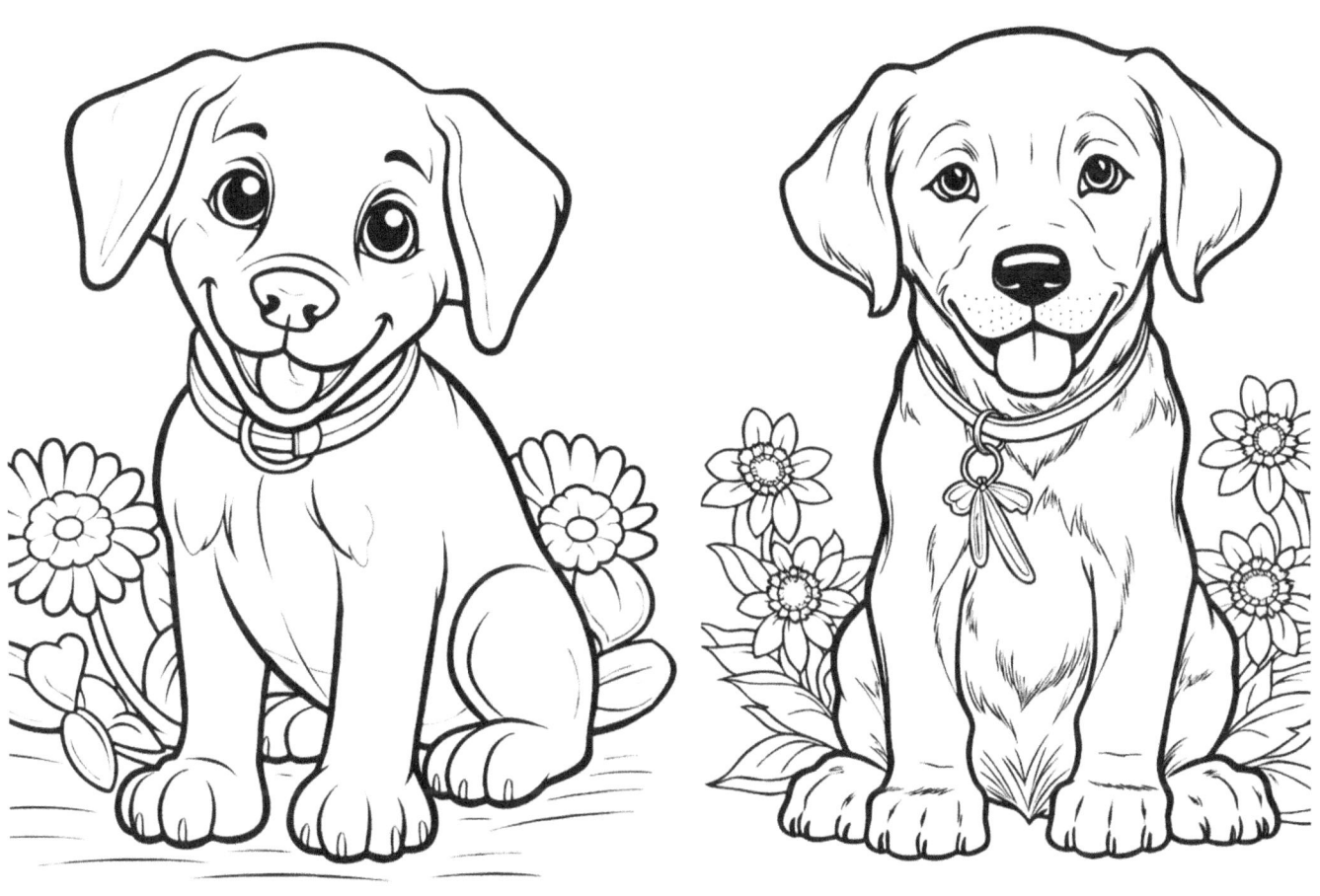

50.

Butterfly

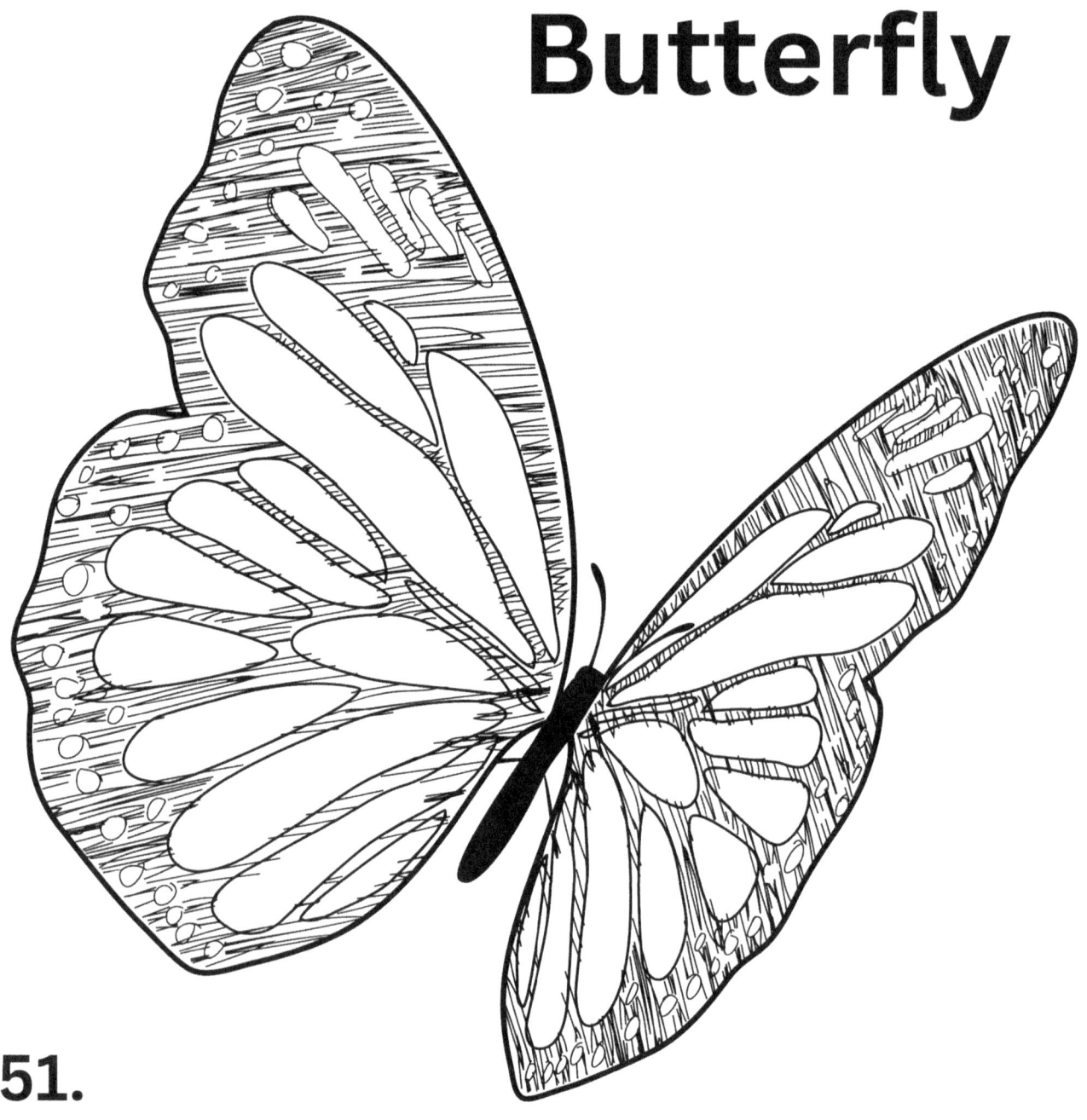

51.

Fish

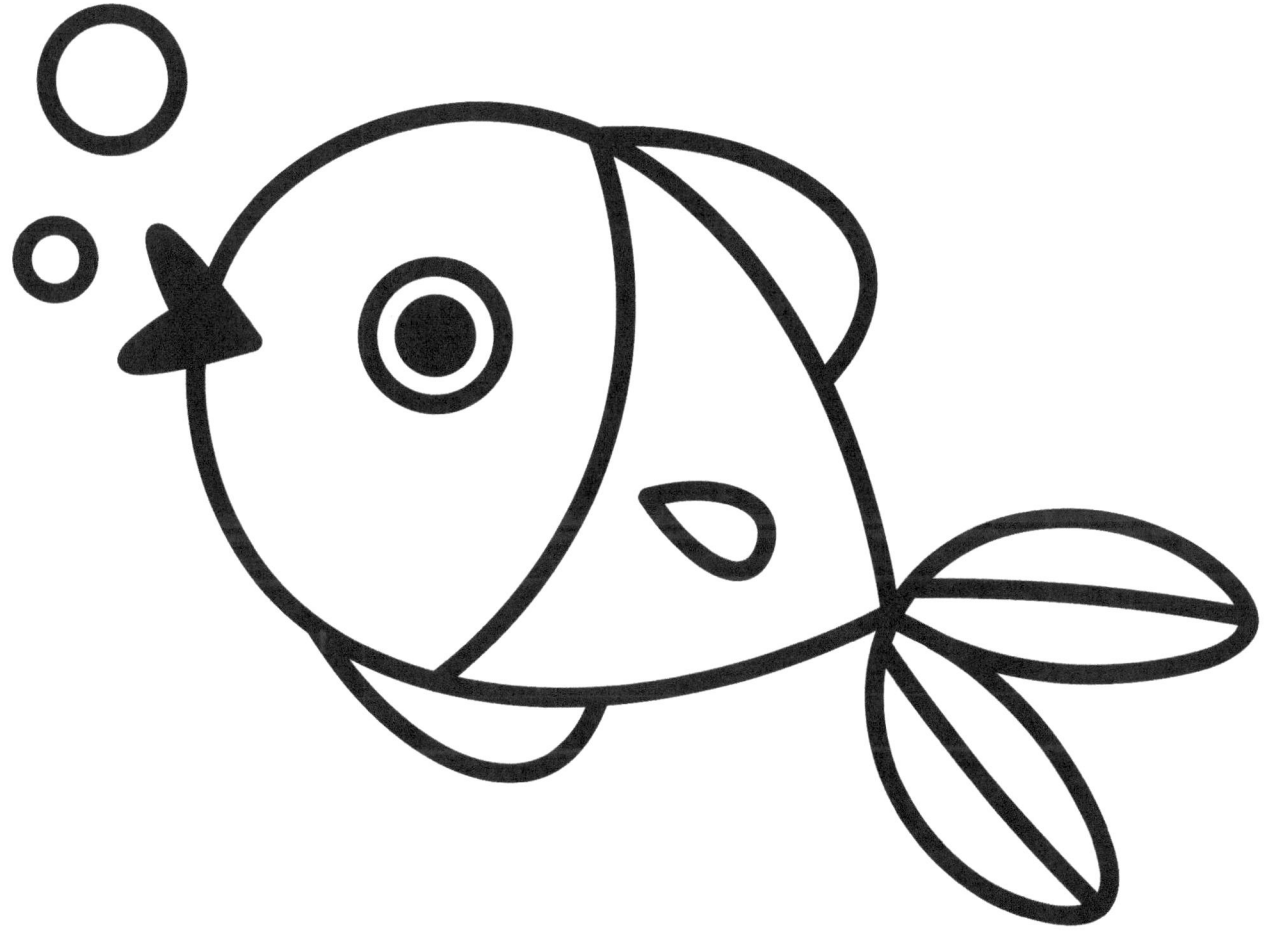

52.

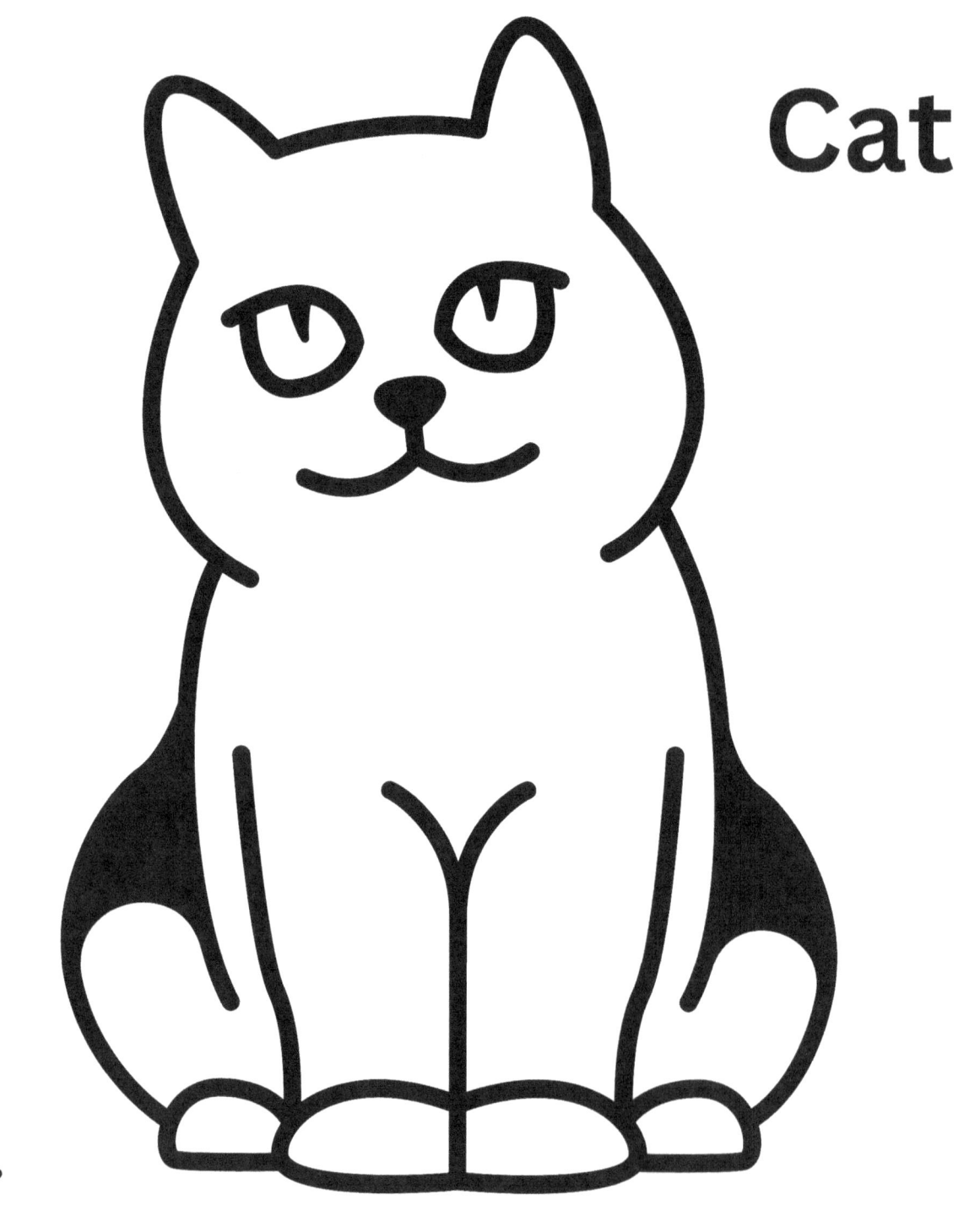

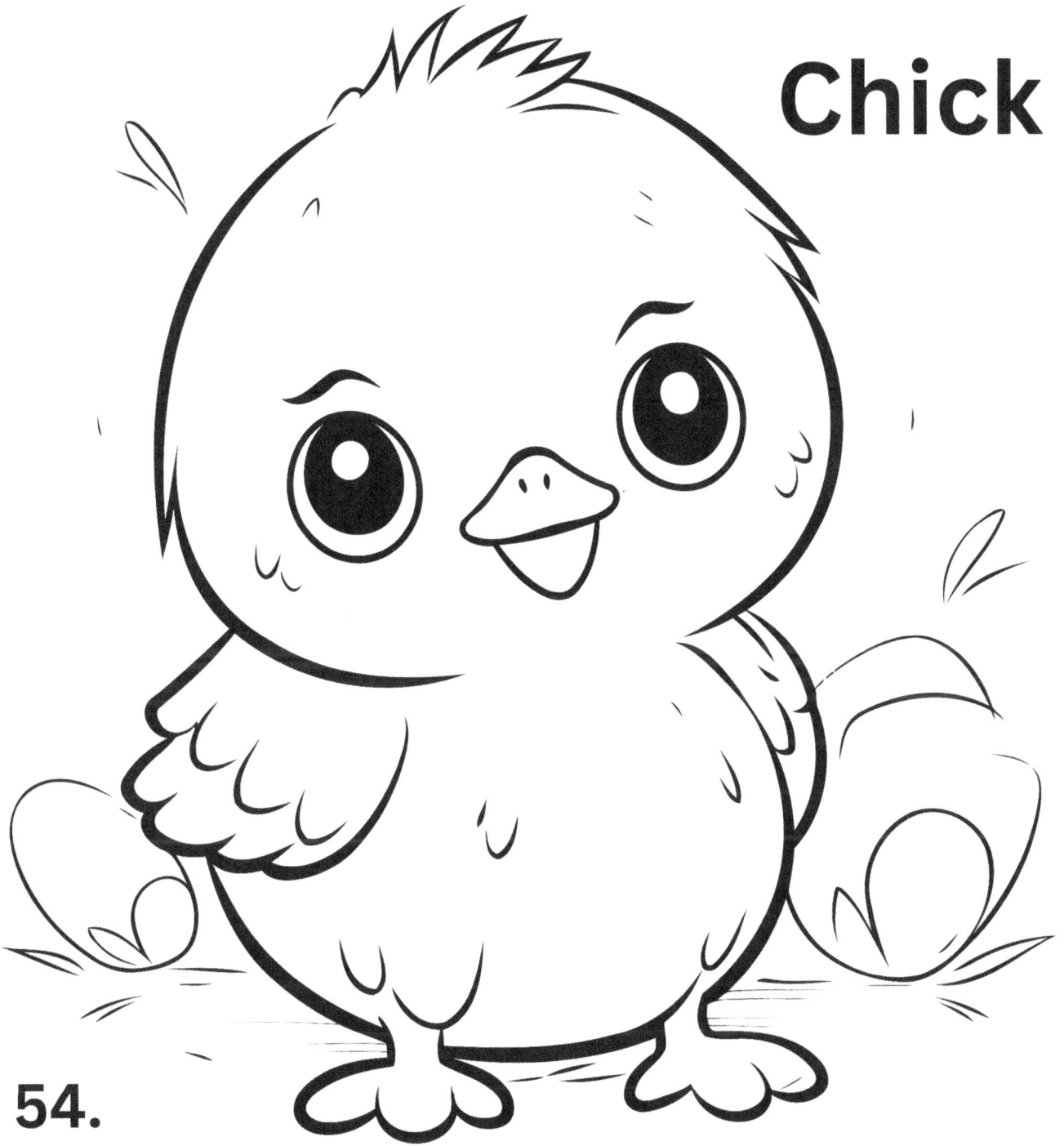

Chick

54.

Crocodile

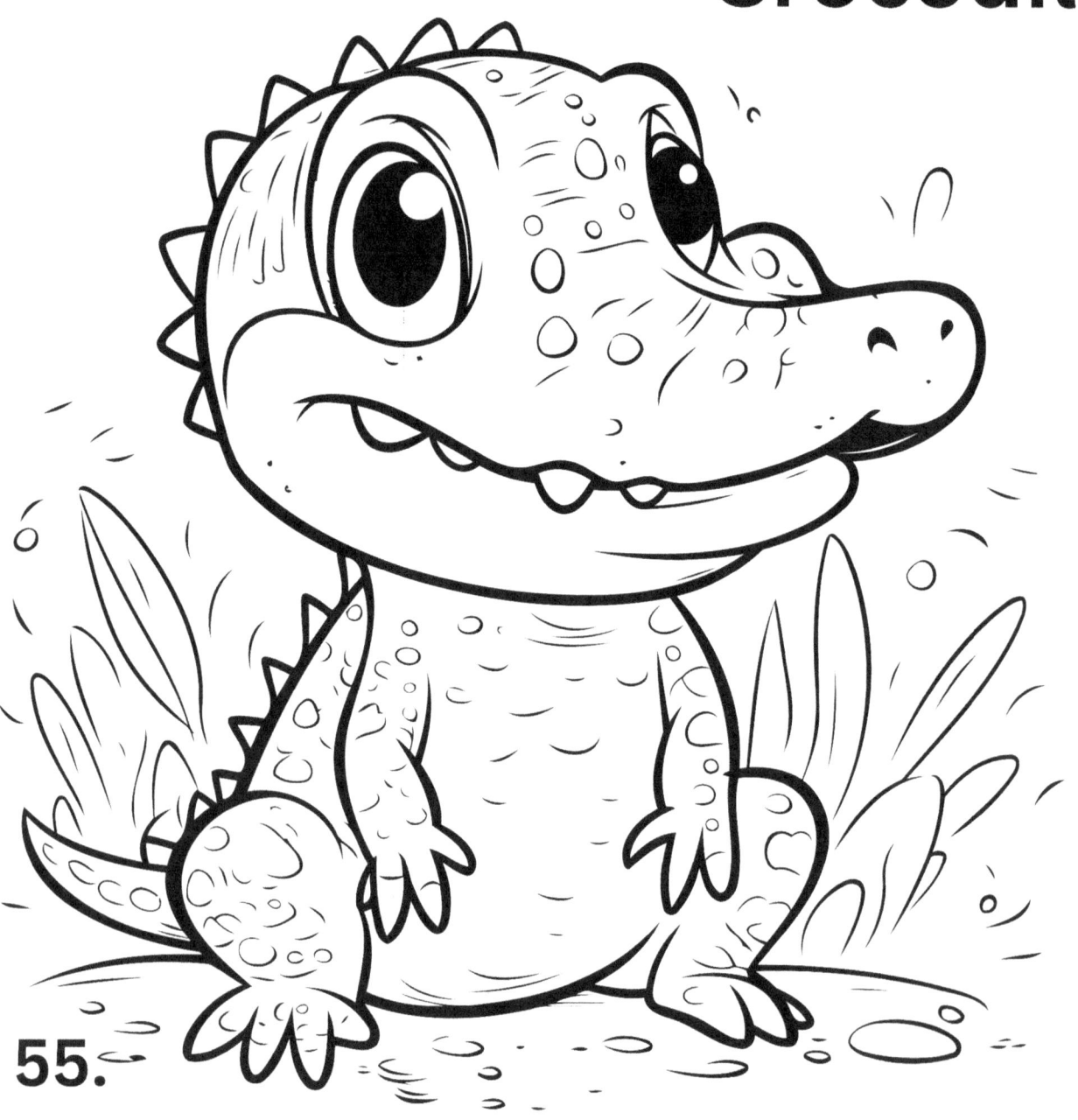

55.

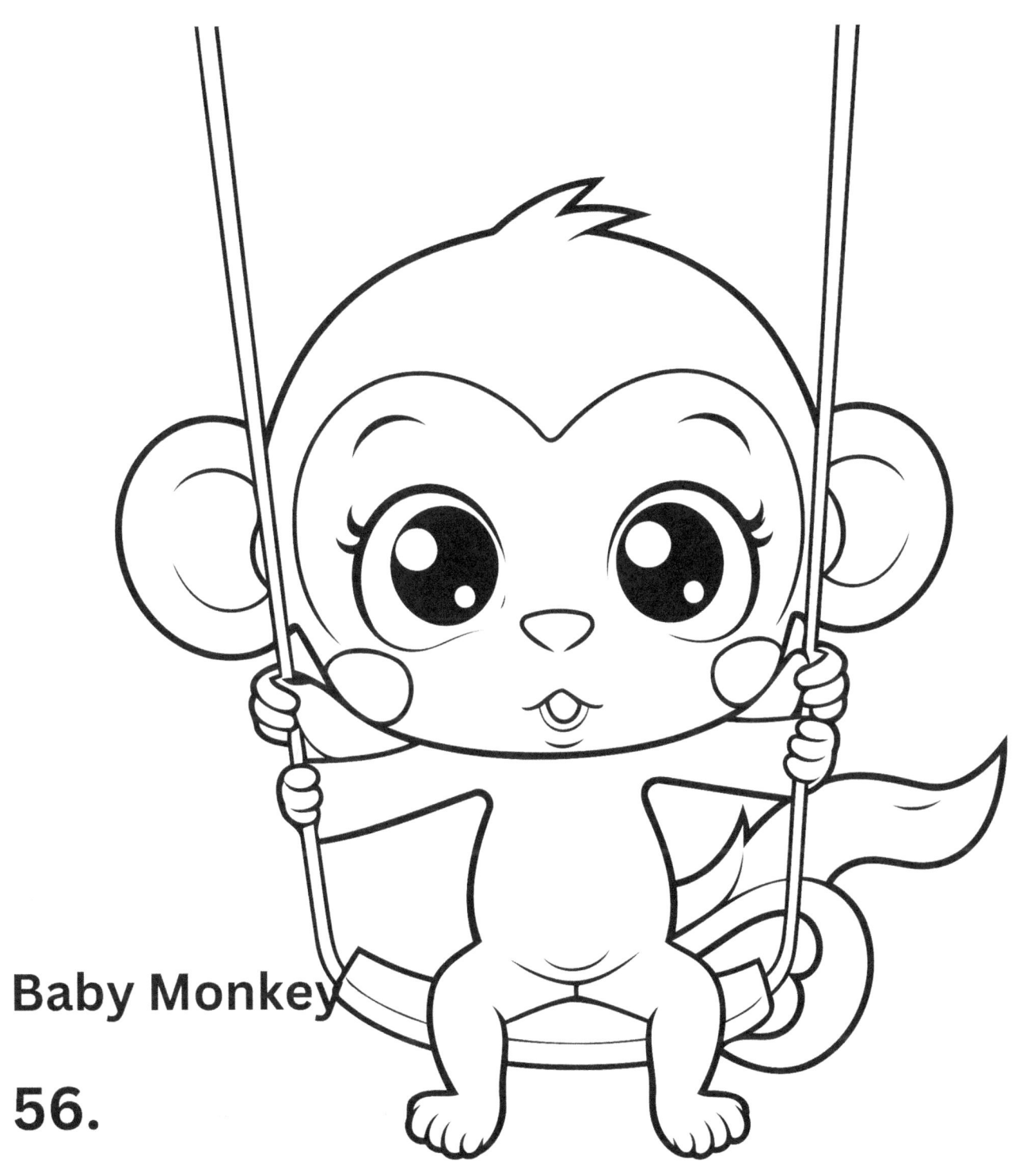

Baby Monkey

56.

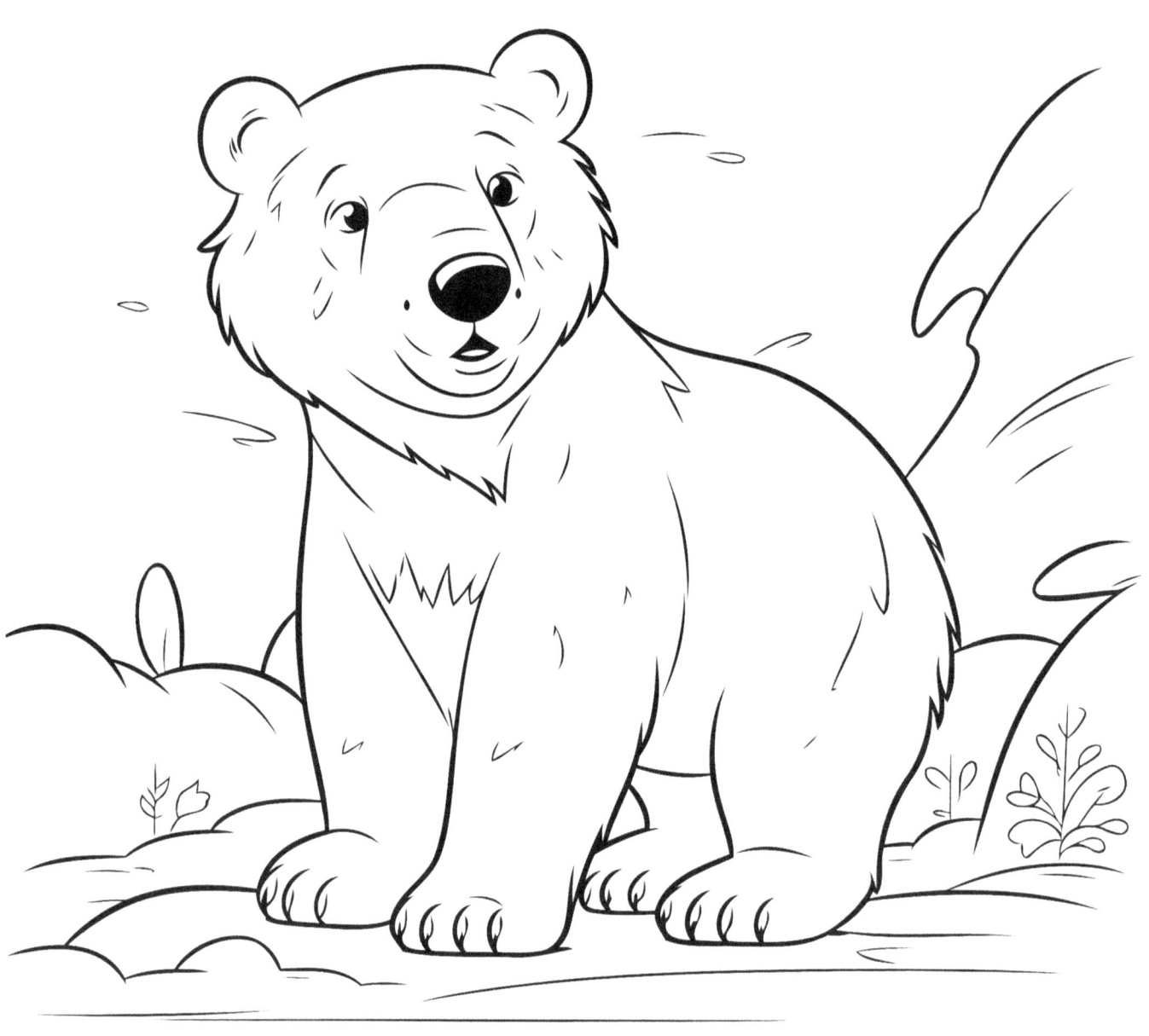

57. **Polar Bear**

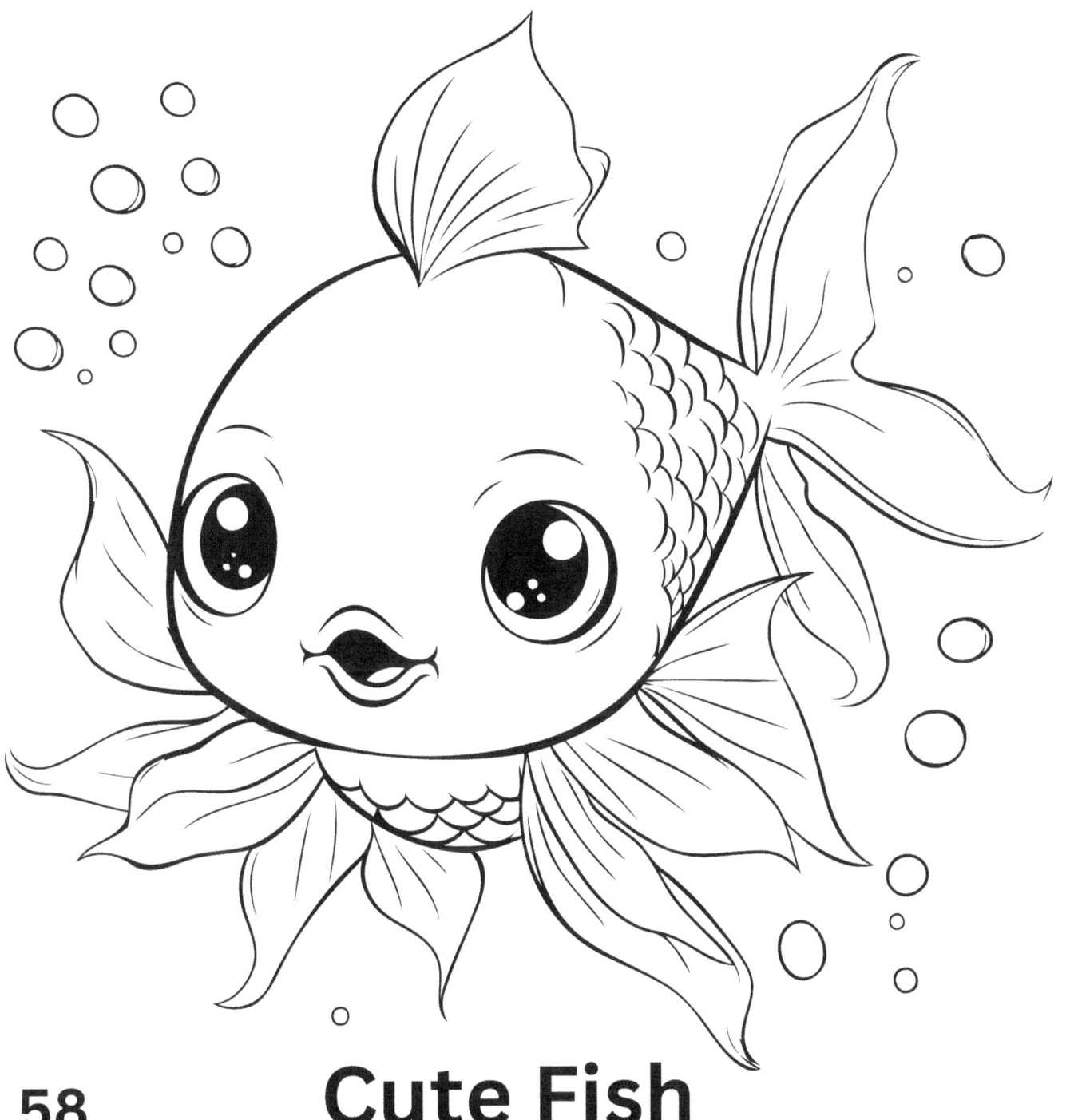

Cute Fish

58.

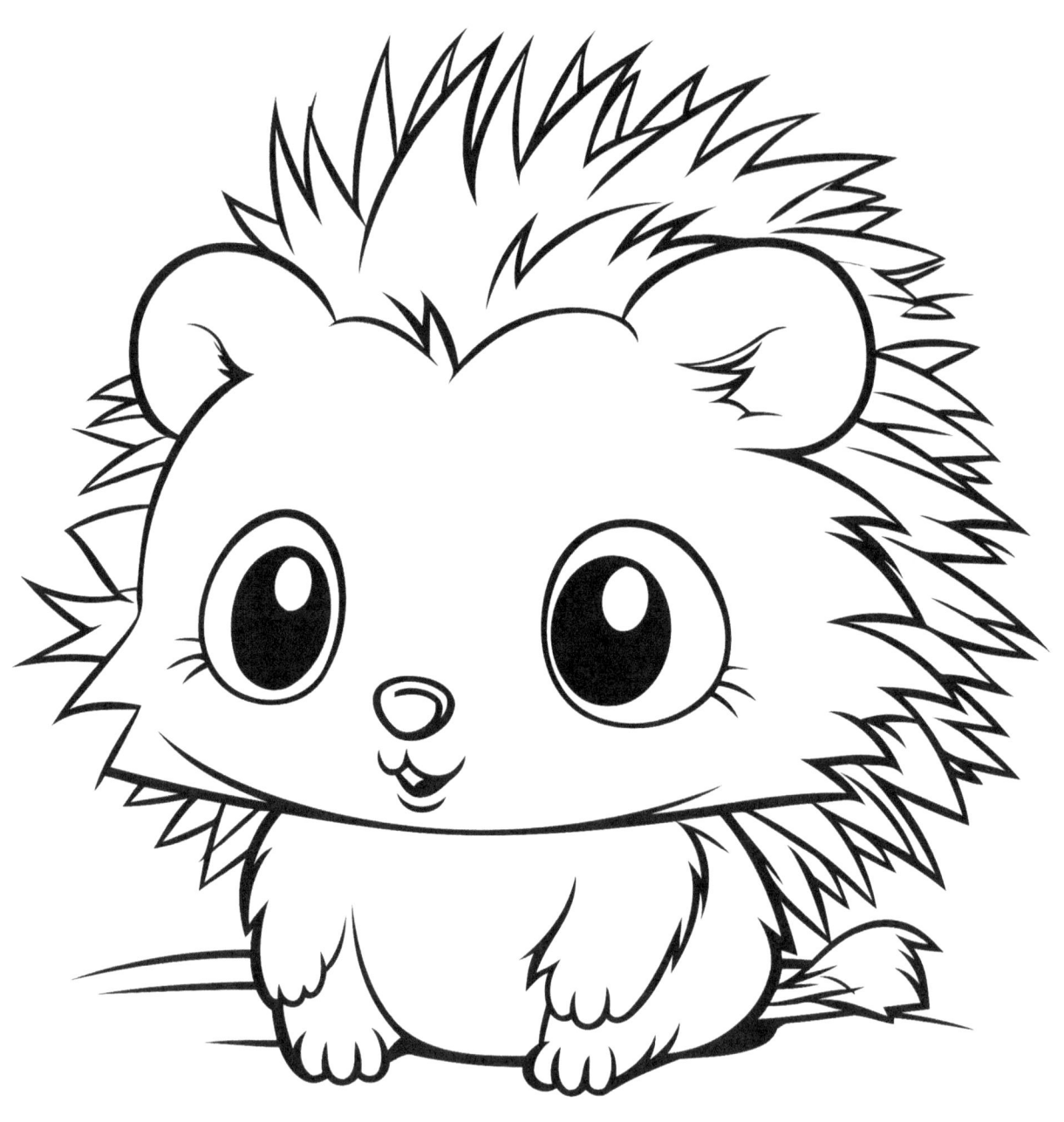

59. **Hedgehog**

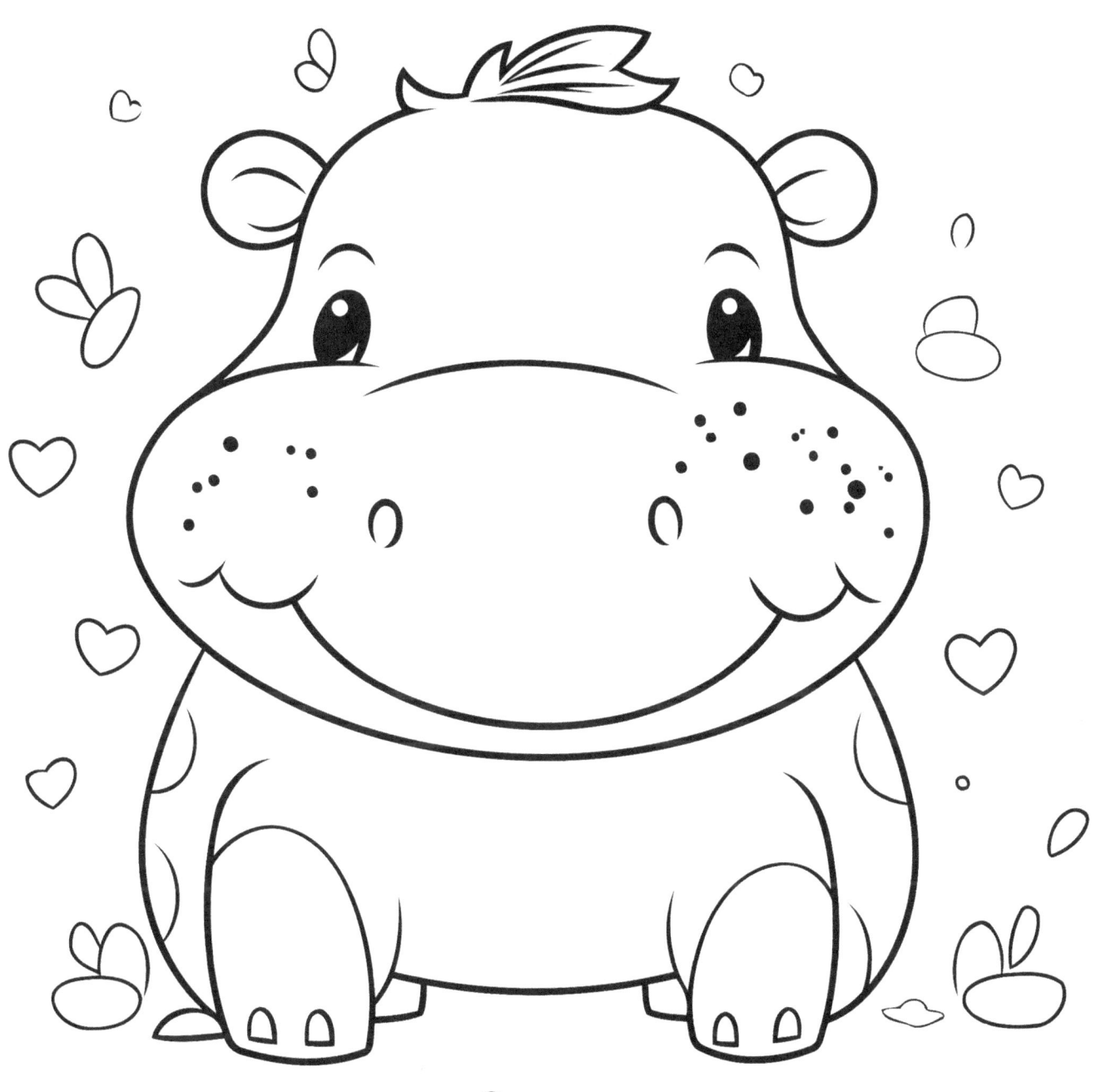

60. **Hippo**

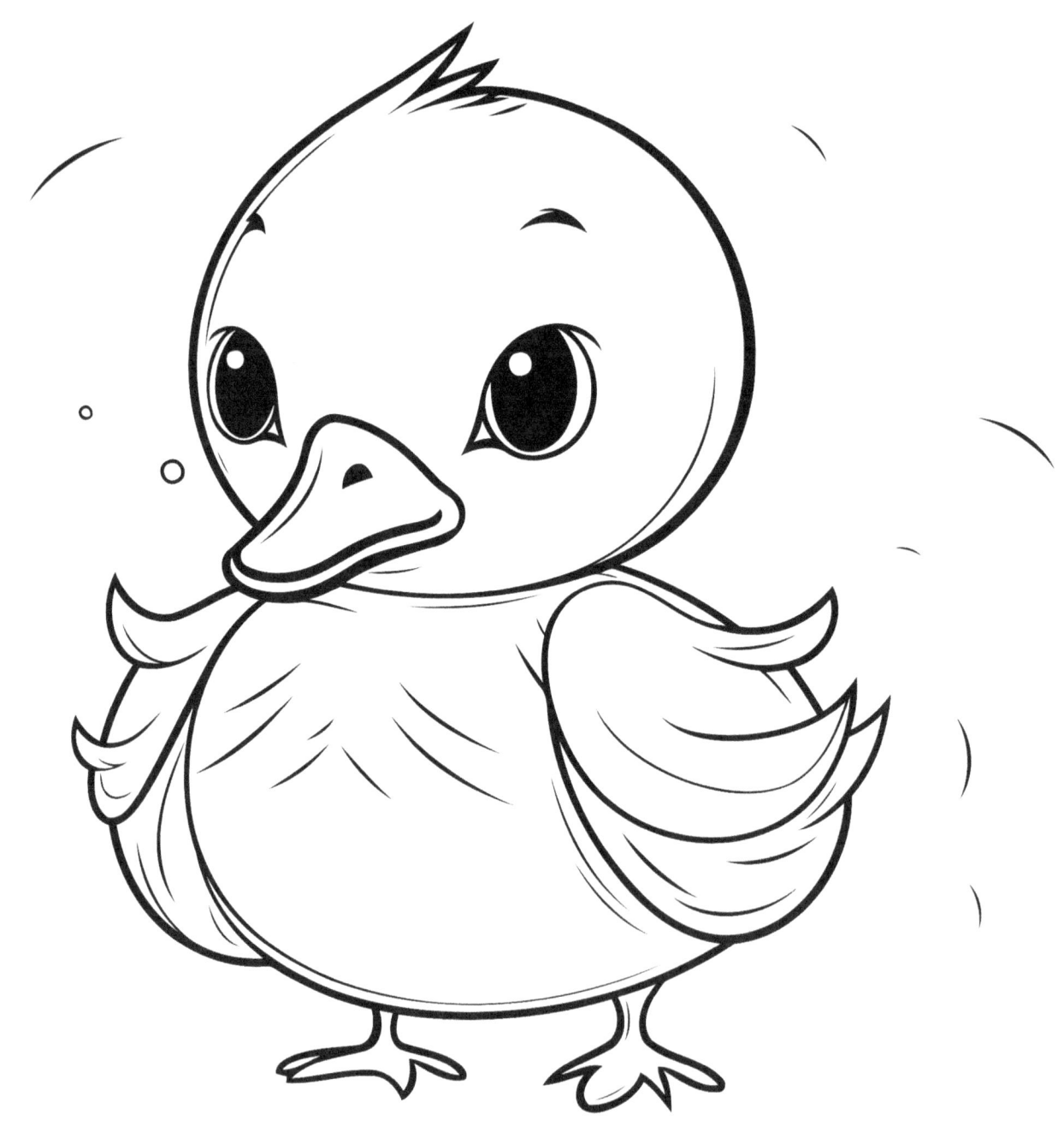

61. **Duckling**

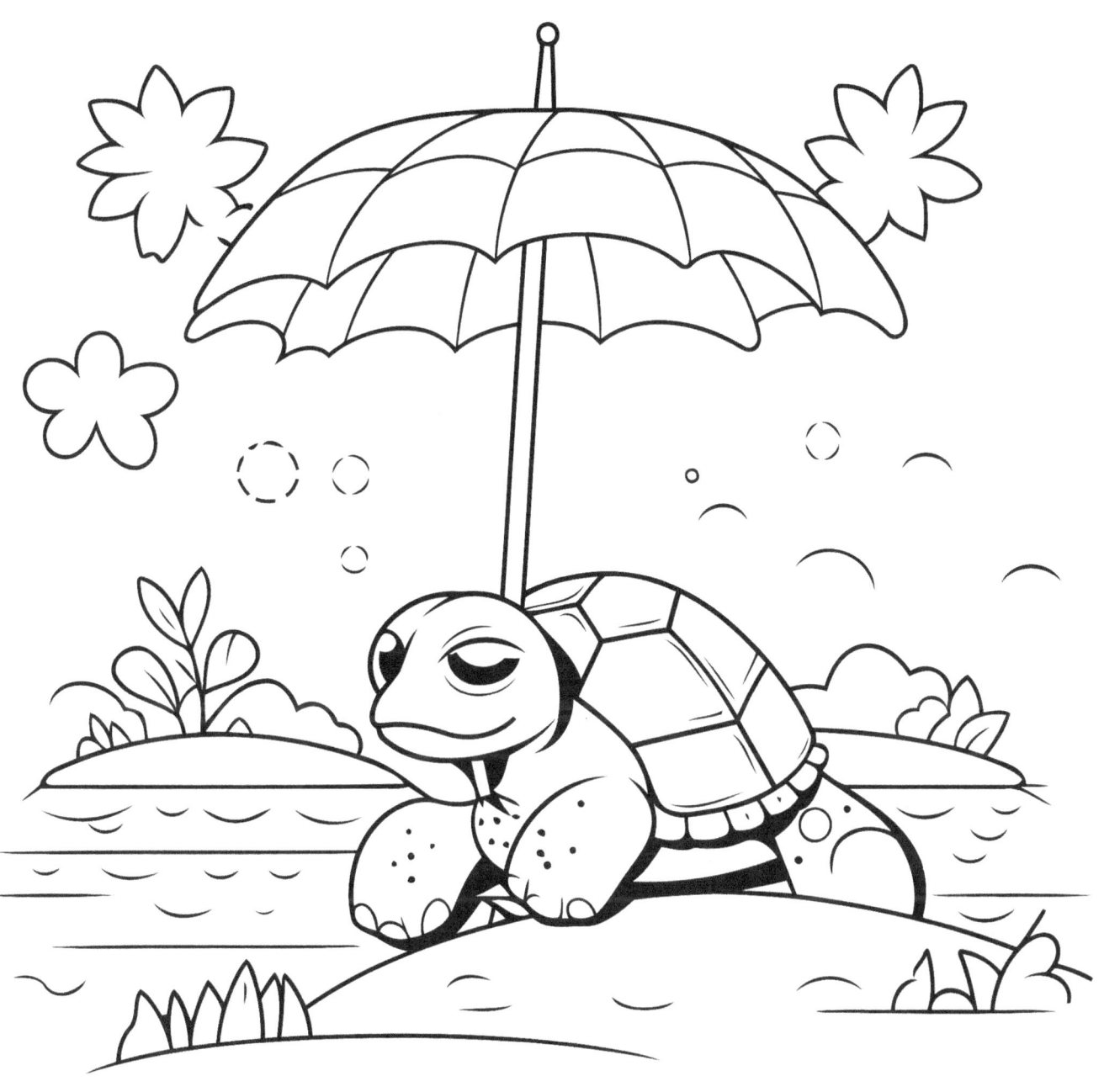

Turtles

62.

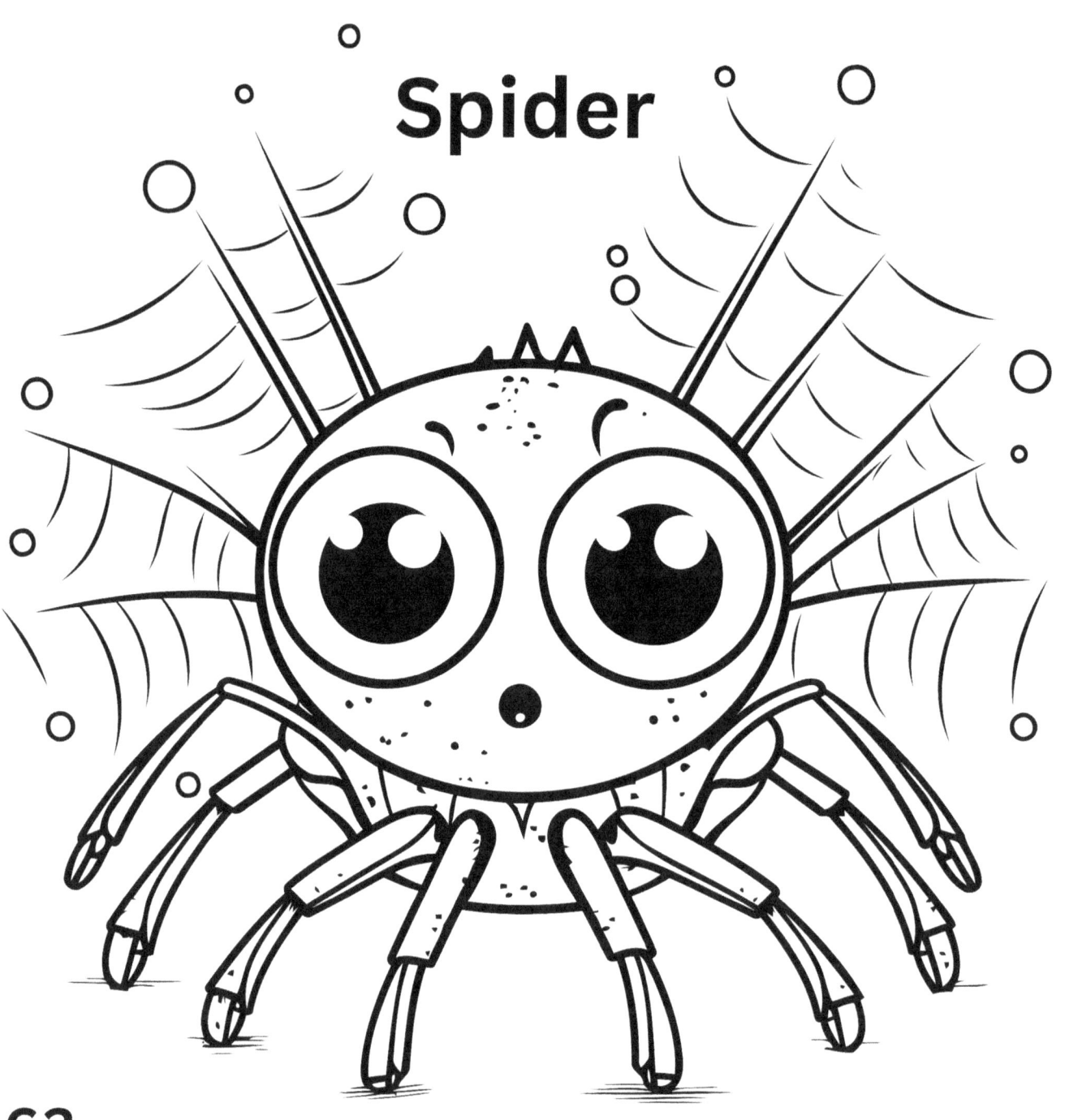

63.

Girl

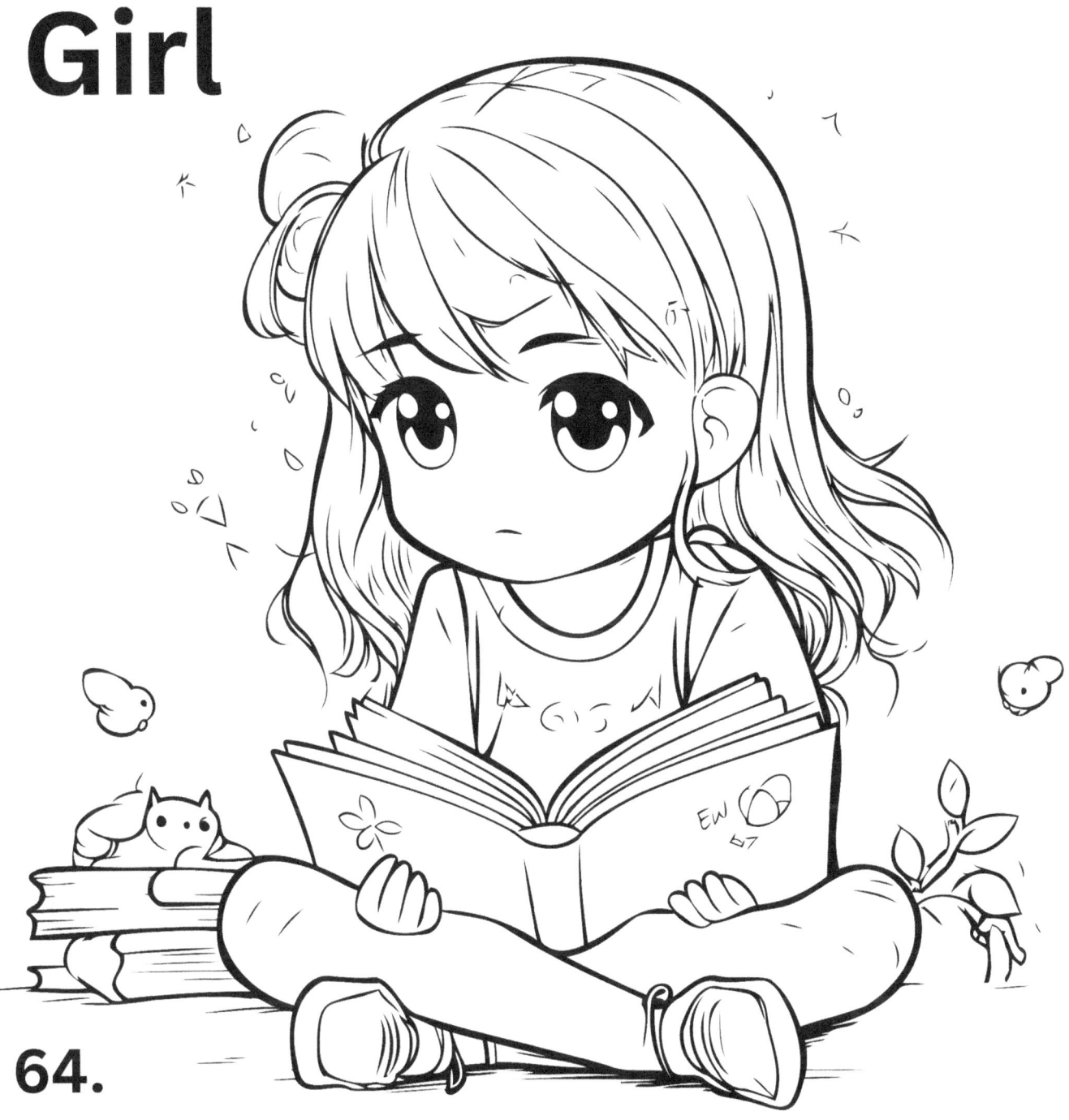

64.

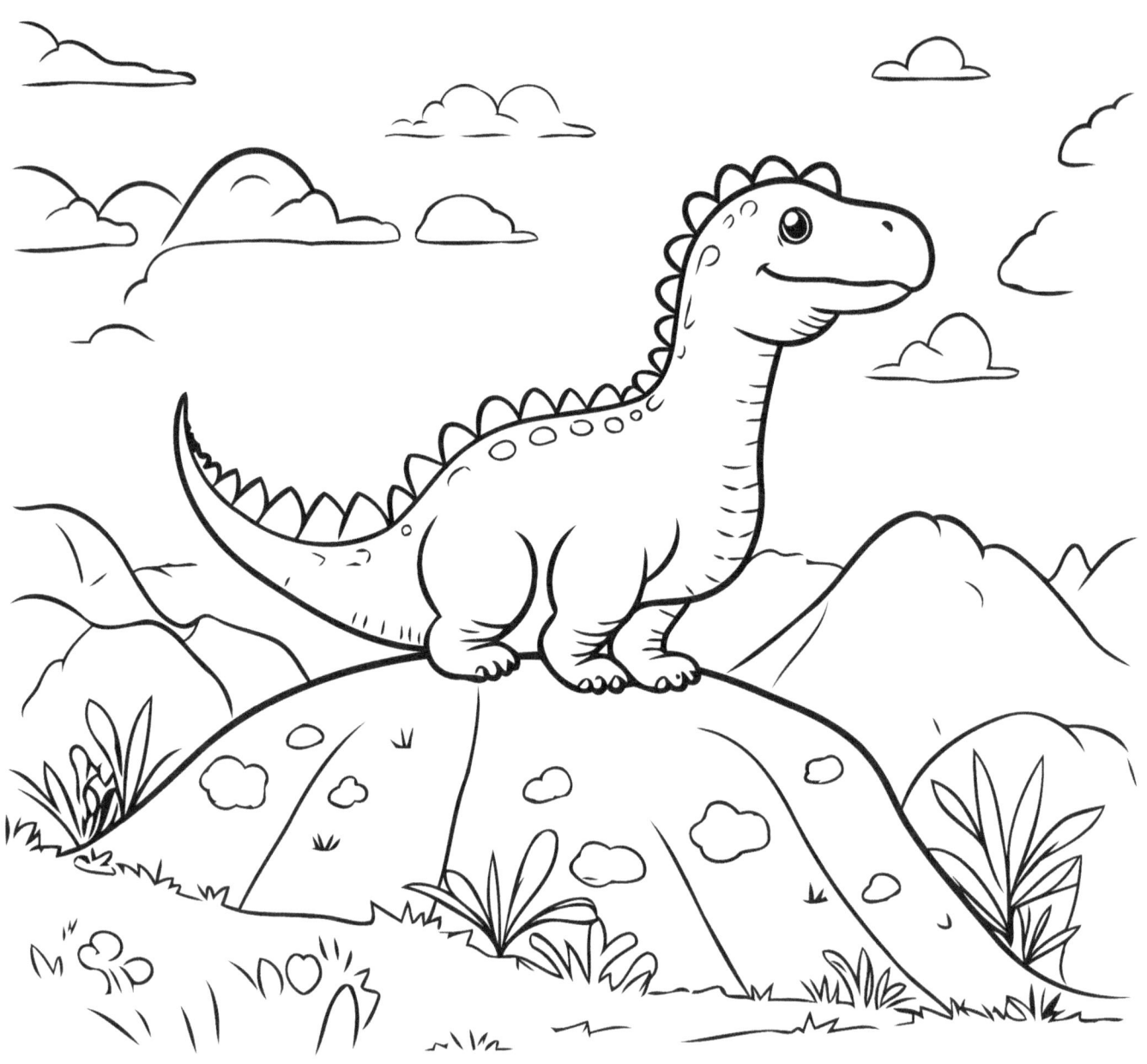

Dinosaur

65.

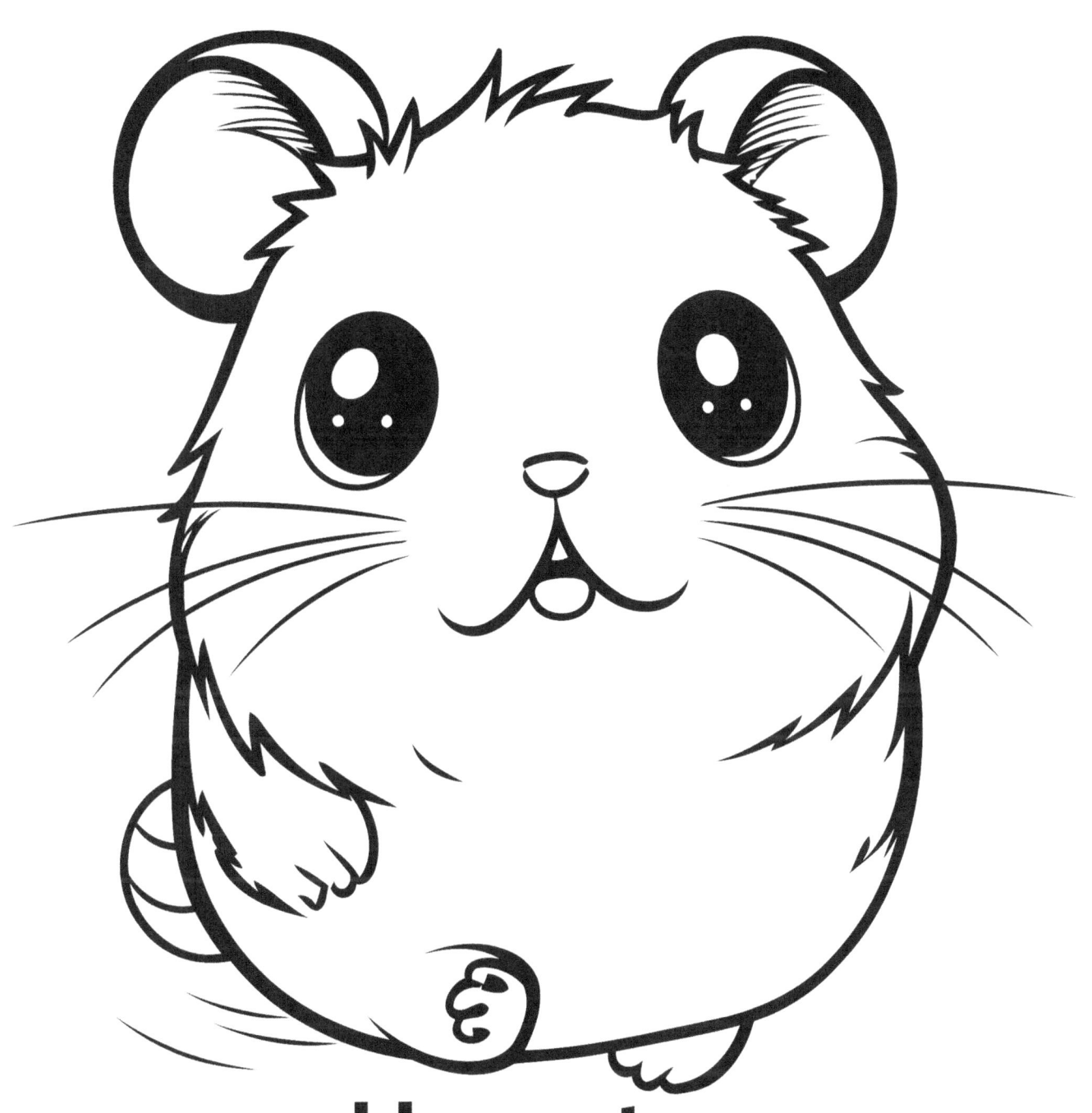

66. **Hamster**

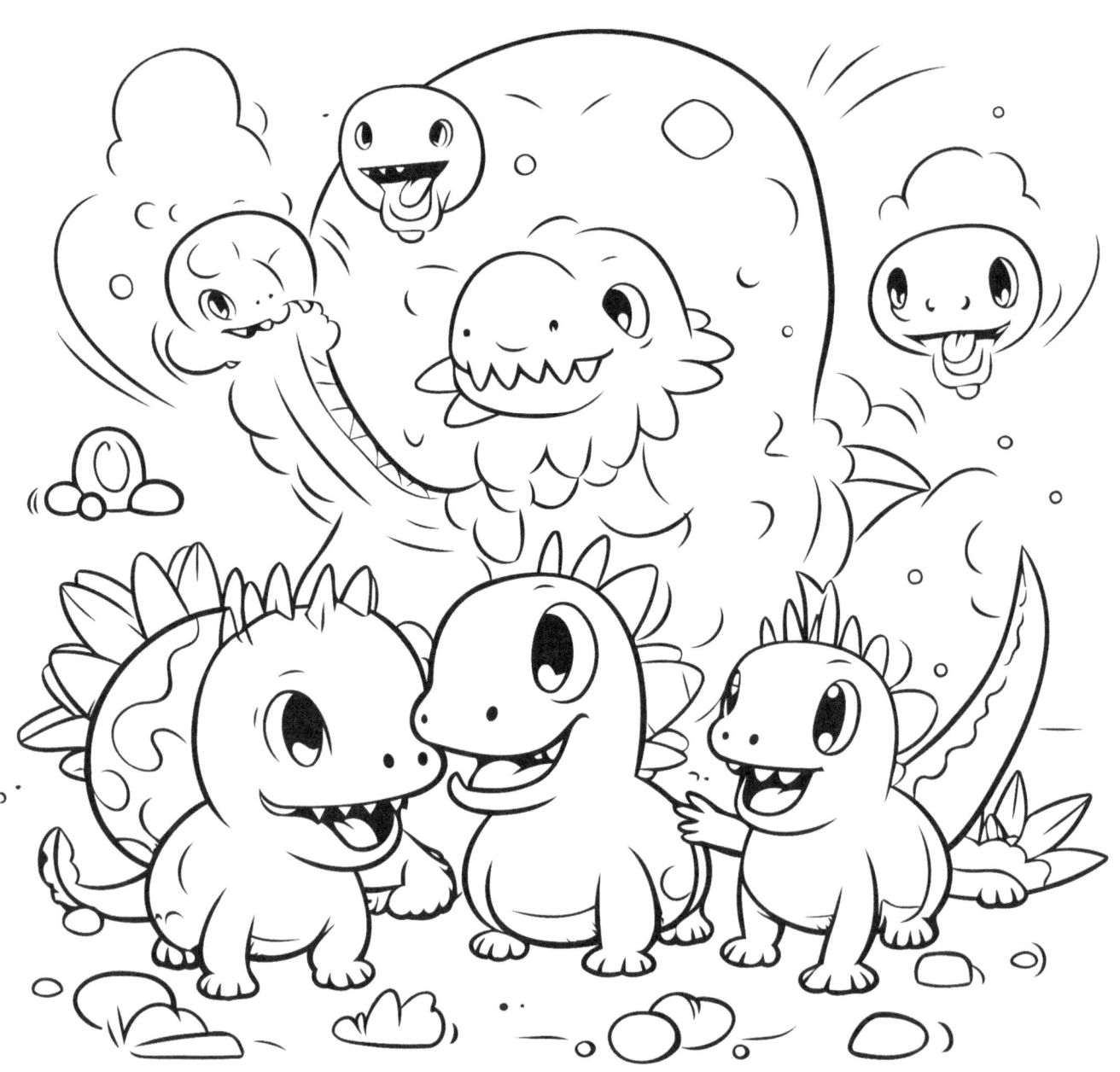

67.   Baby Dinosaur

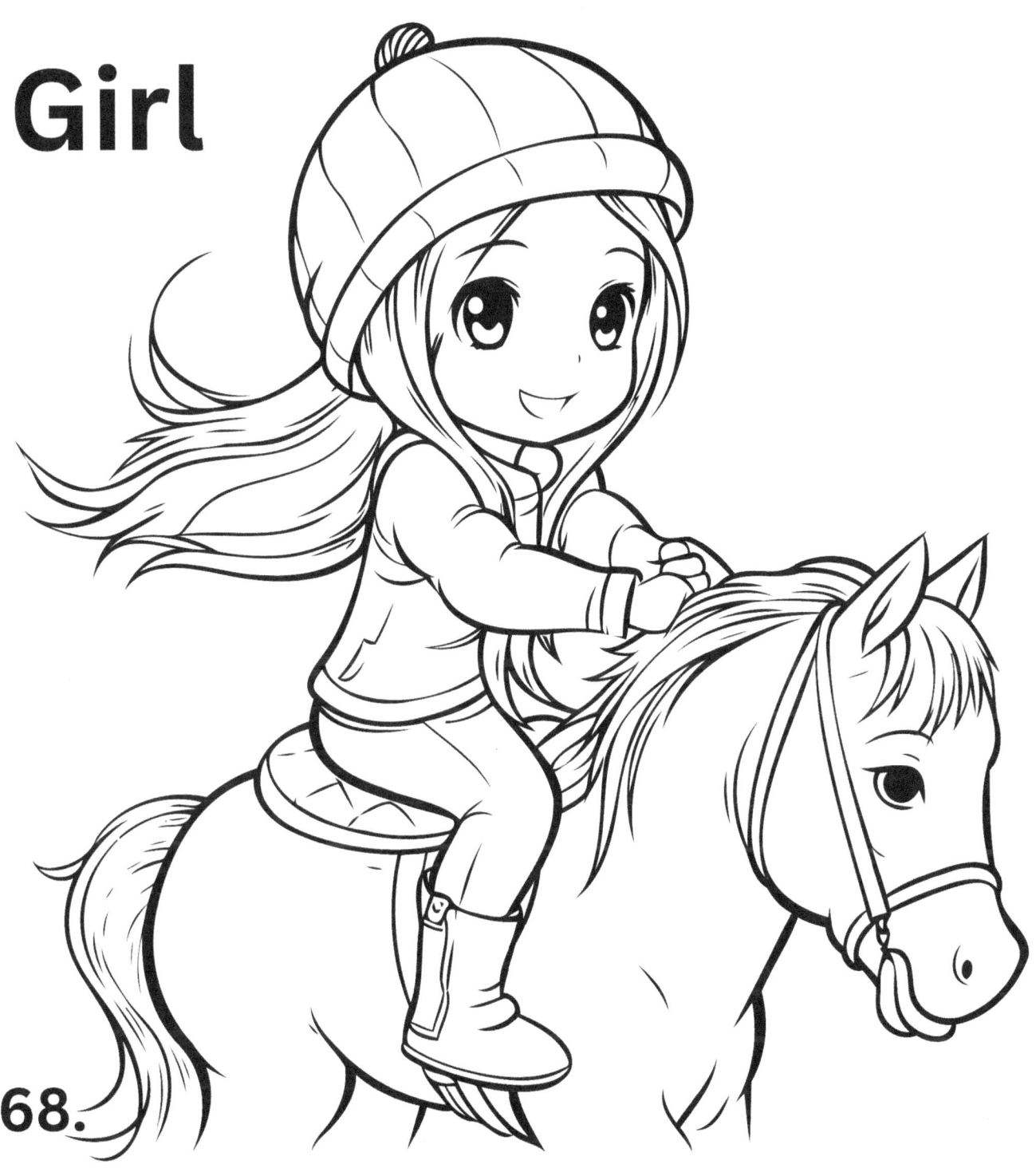

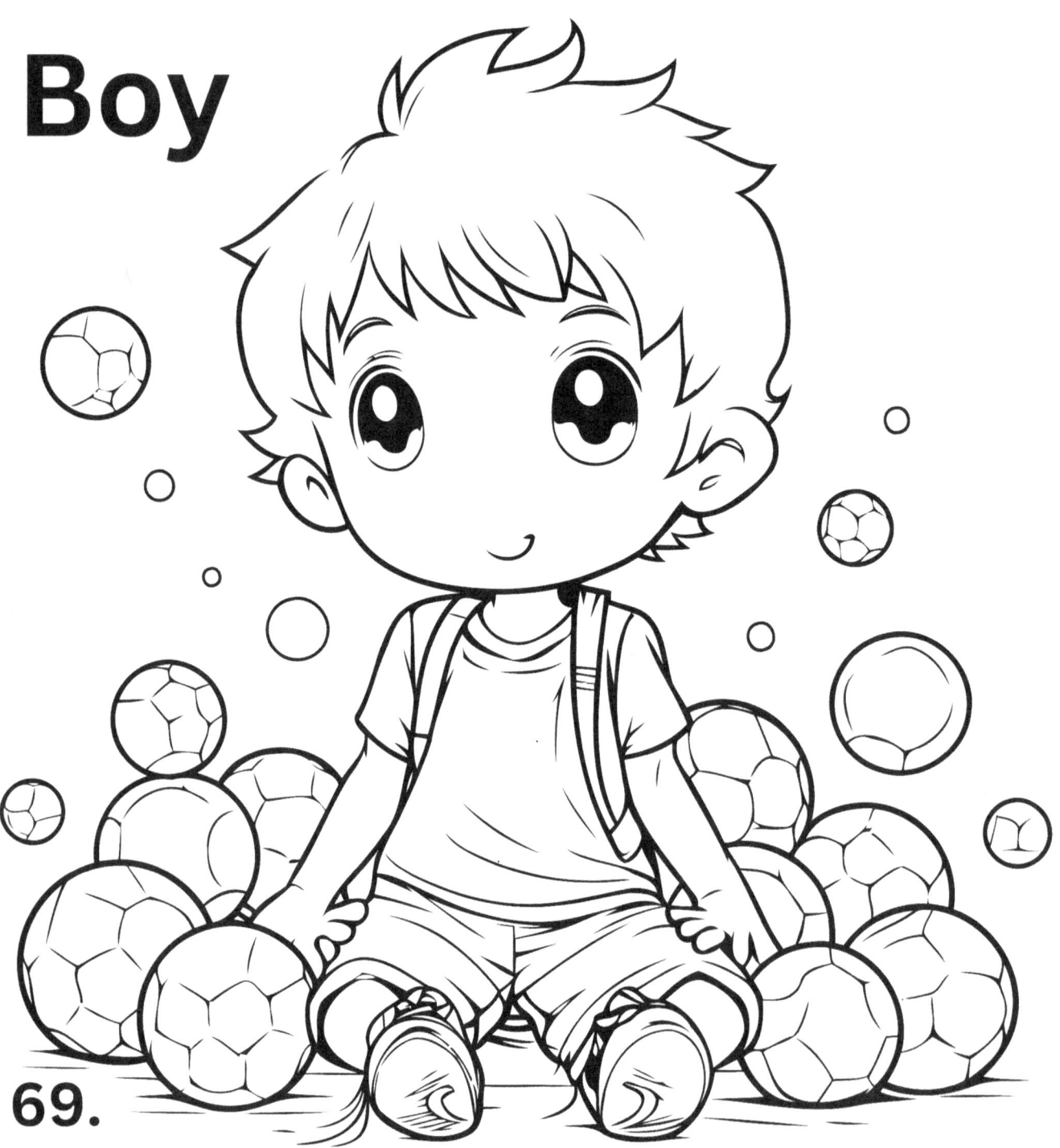

Boy

69.

Boy

70.

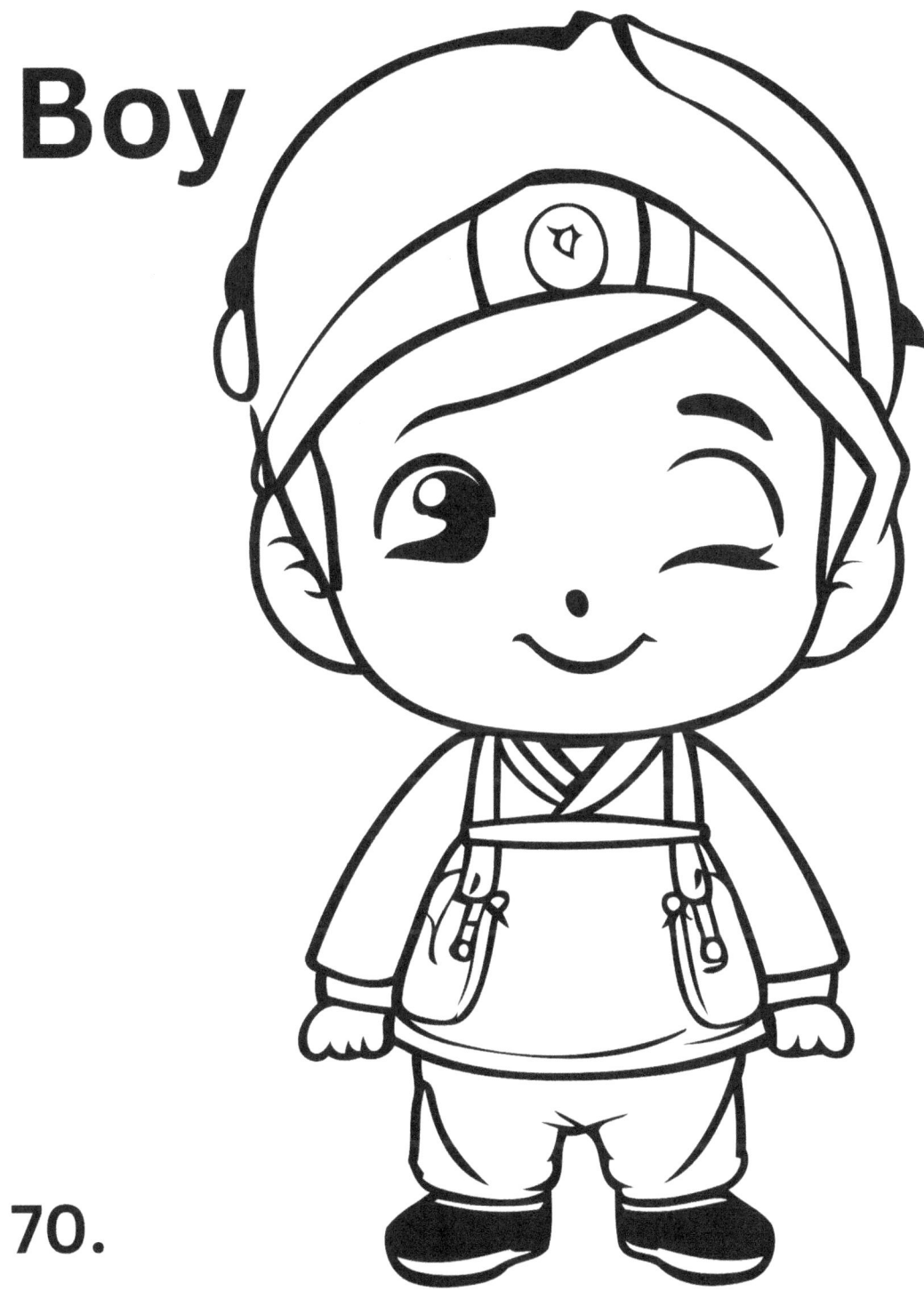

Hope you had fun exploring your creativity!

(Author)- Trevor lloyd Dixon
please check out my other books
on amazon thank u.

72.

73.

www.ingramcontent.com/pod-product-compliance
Lightning Source LLC
Chambersburg PA
CBHW080223220526
45470CB00015B/3189